PASSING STRANGE

PASSING STRANGE

The Complete
Book and Lyrics of the
Broadway Musical

Book and Lyrics by Stew

Music by Stew and Heidi Rodewald

Created in Collaboration with
Annie Dorsen

APPLAUSE
THEATRE & CINEMA BOOKS

An Imprint of Hal Leonard Corporation
New York

Published in 2009 by Applause Theatre & Cinema Books
An Imprint of Hal Leonard Corporation
7777 West Bluemound Road
Milwaukee, WI 53213

Trade Book Division Editorial Offices
19 West 21st Street, New York, NY 10010

Photographs of the original Broadway cast of *Passing Strange*
© 2008 by Carol Rosegg

Printed in the United States of America

Book design by Lesley Kunikis

Library of Congress Cataloging-in-Publication Data
Stew (Musician)
  [Passing strange. Libretto]
  Passing strange : the complete book and lyrics of the Broadway musical /
book and lyrics by Stew ; music by Stew and Heidi Rodewald ; created in
collaboration with Annie Dorsen.
      p. cm.
  ISBN 978-1-55783-752-3 (alk. paper)
  1. Musicals--Librettos. I. Rodewald, Heidi. II. Dorsen, Annie. III. Title.

ML50.S8456P37 2009
782.1'40268--dc22
                              2008055035

www.applausepub.com

For Bibi,
Freya,
Music,
and Miss Irma.

Perhaps the answer was in the songs.

—James Baldwin, *Another Country*

Contents

Foreword

What's inside is just a lie.

No one would have even predicted that Stew's bio might now begin with "Tony Award®–winning playwright Stew, of the cult band The Negro Problem . . ." It all started with a phone call, a proposition, and a lie.

Stew and his collaborator Heidi Rodewald were becoming personal favorites at Joe's Pub at the Public Theater, the intimate, adventurous cabaret space named for Joseph Papp that I had been directing since 2001. A number of friends—Darrell McNeill of the Black Rock Coalition, journalist and filmmaker Jaime Wolf, musician Chocolate Genius—suggested that Joe's Pub would be the perfect place for Stew's "afro-baroque" rock cabaret, and in early 2002, he and Heidi began playing the Pub regularly.

In 2003, I suggested to the Public Theater's then–artistic director George Wolfe that we try to develop a theater piece with Stew and Heidi. Building on the Public's tradition of creating groundbreaking works in non-traditional ways—pieces like *Hair*, *Runaways*, *A Chorus Line* and *Bring in 'da Noise, Bring in 'da Funk*—we were looking for artists who performed at Joe's Pub who might not have had a theater past, but could have a theater future.

Stew seemed like a perfect candidate. His shows had an inherent theatricality with surreal spiels linking songs full of deft wordplay, taut poetic narratives, layers of meaning, and hilariously biting social commentary, all set to his and Heidi's sophisticated, hook-filled melodies.

I remember calling Stew one night to see if he might be interested in getting involved in a festival of new hybrid music/ theater works. I asked if he had ever thought about writing for the theater. "Sure," he said, and told me about a piece he had been developing called *The Hyperion*, about the denizens of a boho coffeehouse turned corporate chain, not unlike what would later appear in his song "Les Arteest Café." He was lying.

Ideas are dependable, there's a new one every week.

Nonetheless, he whipped up a treatment, and we started talking about developing a show. We envisioned bringing in a director to further formalize his concerts into a sort-of multimedia solo performance that would explore the rich world of characters that populated albums like *The Naked Dutch Painter*. The Public's then-dramaturge Rebecca Rugg and I began a process of identifying potential collaborators, including a former Yale associate of Rebecca's, Annie Dorsen. In early 2004, we invited Annie to see Stew's concert at New York's Symphony Space, titled *Stew's Travelogue (of Demonically Energized Souls)*. While no one was told that this was a secret first sketch of a theatricalized Stew show, the *New York Times*' Jon Pareles insightfully observed, "Onstage, Stew was as much an actor as a singer . . . Without cynicism or naïve optimism, he understands human weaknesses and all the fascinating troubles they can cause."

A match had been made, and shortly afterward the Public commissioned Stew, Heidi and Annie for their first workshop. It wasn't a lot of money—what Annie would refer to as a "ghetto commission"—which allowed the workshop to be fairly low risk. Not only had Stew never actually written a play before, but the number of shows he claimed to have seen could be counted on one hand. So we went into the workshop without specific expectations; we just wanted to give three talented artists a chance to play. Like a garage-band jam session, they could try out different material, get to know each other, see if the idea of creating a show around Stew's songs and stories had any potential, and discover whether it might be possible to find a meeting place between a rock show and a theater piece.

They sat in a rehearsal room at the Public and spoke about cosmographies and travel and art and what makes a rock show great. Stew brought in fragments of writings and poems and sketches of songs, which Annie helped to shape and structure into a theatrical arc, originally conceived of as a three-part journey—Los Angeles, Europe (Amsterdam and Berlin) and a return "home" to the void of the youth's mother's death in L.A. Some of that very first writing has endured in the script that follows.

> Sometimes, the melody's going one way,
> but then the song has other plans.

Not long afterward, *Passing Strange* was submitted to the Sundance Institute, which invited the trio of creators to their Theater Lab that summer. Given concentrated creative time, a (multiethnic) cast of actors to play with and seasoned theater professionals to give feedback, Stew, Heidi and Annie began to reshape the show into an ensemble piece, which became the hit of the Theater Lab. If he was lying when he first told us that he was writing a play, the lie was turning into the truth.

Among the theater people who got to see this presentation at Sundance were Oskar Eustis, then artistic director of Trinity Rep in Providence, and Les Waters of Berkeley Rep in California, who were both interested in involving their theaters in the show. Later that year, when Oskar replaced George Wolfe as artistic director of the Public, he made *Stew's Travelogue* (now redubbed *Passing Strange*) a priority.

> *Unannounced you've grown*
> *Into a living thing*

Stew, Heidi and Annie continued developing the show through numerous workshops. They introduced new songs from the show at gigs in Joe's Pub and elsewhere, including a 2004 show at the Delacorte Theater, home of the Public's Shakespeare in Central Park. In 2005, Berkeley Rep, under the leadership of Tony Taccone, came aboard as a co-producer. That summer, Stew, Heidi, Annie and the band returned for a rare second visit to the Sundance Theater Lab, where their cast included Daniel Breaker, who quickly owned the role of the Youth. The Public then partnered with Stanford University's Institute for Creativity in the Arts for a residency in which Annie Dorsen staged the complete show for the first time, working in collaboration with "movement coordinator" Karole Armitage.

For the first time, the show featured an all-black cast—including de'Adre Aziza and Chad Goodridge—both clarifying some of the show's incisive commentary on racial identity and raising provocative new questions. When the staff of the Public and Berkeley Rep saw the show in early 2006 in front of an audience for the first time at Stanford, it became clear that something truly original was being created. A rock concert that told a story, rich with humor and pain. One that could kick out the jams and then rip your heart from your chest when you weren't paying attention. And to quote one of Stew's fan-favorite songs, "Rehab," we were "very, very, very, very, very, very, very, very, very, very, very optimistic."

Following that successful workshop, the show opened in October 2006 at Berkeley Rep, where the rest of what became the Broadway cast—Eisa Davis, Rebecca Naomi Jones and Colman Domingo—filled out the ensemble. The Berkeley production won broad acclaim, including a Bay Area Critics Circle Award for Best Ensemble, and buzz began generating for the New York premiere. It was clear that Stew was indeed a playwright, and a damn good one at that.

> *I am no mere* popsongmaker. *I am an artist.*
> *My work is about re-invention.*
> *My work is about . . . transcendence. My work is about . . .*
> *the limits of blackness.*

After another series of workshops, edits and rewrites, *Passing Strange* opened in the Public's Anspacher Theater in May 2007 to even more rave reviews. In *The New Yorker*, Hilton Als exclaimed: "Not since Stephen Sondheim introduced a kind of Jewish skepticism and irony to the Broadway musical, in the nineteen-fifties, and Tony Kushner revolved his 2003 show, *Caroline, or Change*, around the ways in which class intersects with race have we had such a finely crafted, ethnic-minded American musical as *Passing Strange*." That year, *Passing Strange* joined 2006–2007's Tony and Pulitzer Prize winners in the prestigious *Best Plays Theater Yearbook*, and the production later earned numerous awards, including two Obies and four Audelcos.

The momentum built, and in the space of a short two-month run, fans returned two, three, four and more times with friends in tow. They became ambassadors for a hard-to-describe show that told a universal story of a youth coming of age, searching for truth and meaning—The Real—through the very particular "autobiographical fiction" lens of a black middle-class-cum-bohemian rock musician. Fans included venerable Broadway producers Elizabeth McCann and Gerald Schoenfeld of the Shubert Organization, who, along with executive producer Joey Parnes, saw true possibilities for this maverick show to make its way to Broadway. A concert of songs from the show at the 2007 Joe's Pub in the Park series had the cast being received like rock stars, and somehow this theater piece that had started as a rock show had found its way back home, while at the same time pointing to its next stage.

Broadway seemed like a long shot. *Passing Strange* was an unconventional hybrid of ensemble theater piece and rock concept album come to life, a first play by an underground black rock musician with an all-black cast and experimentalist director, layered with complex themes about the mutability of racial identity, what it means to be an artist, the love between a mother and a son, a search for self and a search for home. It wasn't based on a hit animated movie, wasn't afraid to fill its lyrically dense book with allusions to French arthouse cinema or German industrial artnoise or expatriate artists like James Baldwin and Josephine Baker or suburban black middle class life, and didn't try to wrap its story up in a happy little bow at the end.

At this point in the play we were planning a show tune!
An upbeat "gotta leave this town" kinda show tune!
But we don't know how to write those kinds of tunes . . .

On February 28, 2008, *Passing Strange* opened to praise even more rapturous than it had in its Berkeley and Public incarnations. The critical consensus was almost uniformly positive, with an excitement that theater was being reinvigorated by an original new voice. Continued rewrites, edits, and changes large and small had tightened the show, clarified character relationships, and added even more emotional impact, all the while holding on to its iconoclastic essence. Word of mouth was strong, with new fans from all walks of life, die-hard Broadway lovers and lifelong Broadway skeptics, coming back again and again. Groupies who returned multiple times to experience a catharsis more common to a rock show than a Broadway show dubbed themselves "Passing Strangers" or "Scaryotypes."

Continuing to invent its own rules as it went along, *Passing Strange* recorded its cast album live for Ghostlight/Sh-K-Boom in front of an audience at its home in the Belasco Theater to capture some of the cathartic energy of the performances on stage. The acclaim kept coming, along with many nominations and awards, including ones from Drama Desk and the New York Drama Critics' Circle. The show was nominated for seven Tony Awards, winning one for Best Book of a Musical.

America can't handle freaky Negroes.

Unfortunately, in the world of Broadway, a brilliant show and widespread popular and critical enthusiasm isn't enough to keep a show open, and without winning the "big" prize—the Best Musical Tony—the producers were finding it difficult to translate the show's multiple strengths to the mass audience needed to fuel ticket sales. Filmmaker Spike Lee, who had become a fan at the Public, enthusiastically announced he would film the show in front of an audience, hoping that the buzz would generate a jump in attendance. Unfortunately, not long after, the producers posted the closing notice.

As luck would have it, the performances that Spike would film would end up being the closing weekend. The film captured the ecstatic audience response that finally reached the unbridled energy of a full-on rock show, coupled with the raw emotion of the performers at the end of a journey cut short prematurely.

How you gonna deal?
Right when it was starting to feel real?

In its five-year journey from a beginning as a casually tossed-off lie to an ironic end as a multiple-award-winning Broadway musical, *Passing Strange* became an inspiration to many. To young people who identified with the story of a youth who takes the brave (or reckless) step to leave home to reinvent himself and follow his dreams. To audiences who found an antidote to the malaise of incuriousness that can overwhelm popular culture. To artists who saw that it was still possible to reinvent tired forms and infuse them with a sense of mischievous adventure, intellect and heart.

Too bad it takes so long to see what you've been missing.

It has been said that while only a few hundred people originally bought the Velvet Underground's first album, every person who did started a band. *Passing Strange* didn't have a chance to reach as large an audience as it deserved in the theater. But now that its songs have been preserved in a cast album, the production preserved as a Spike Lee joint, and the text preserved in this book, audiences will continue to be able to take this journey to deal with The Real. And perhaps, some of them will one day lie about that play that they are working on . . .

If it were any more real, baby—
It'd be fiction . . .

—Bill Bragin
Director of Joe's Pub at the Public Theater, 2001–2007
Instigator

Preface

This play wasn't meant to go to Broadway. It was something we were working on in between going on tours and spending time in the studio recording and doing what we could to pay the bills and keep the band going.

When I joined the rock band The Negro Problem back in 1997, I knew it was possible this kind of extraordinary thing could happen. But that's not why you join a band. I joined Stew's band because if we drove ten hours to play at a club with only five people in the audience, which is what you sometimes do in a rock band, I wanted to love the music we were playing. And I did.

This musical has had so many lives with so many different people involved, and just like a rock band, the show we did back at the workshops at Sundance and Stanford, or the opening at Berkeley Rep, or in New York at the Public Theater, all the way to Broadway, was never the same. And it was never about just making it "better." It was just changing, and I love what we ended up with at every stage of its life. Just like a rock band, the show is never going to stay the same. Musicians don't do that.

The reason I think we ended up on Broadway was that Stew, Annie Dorsen and I never wanted to do anything that resembled something you'd normally see there. Because that's never what we wanted. To be on Broadway. But we ended up doing what we'd want to see on Broadway. That's all you can do. Because if no one shows up, you want to love what you're doing.

—Heidi Rodewald

Introduction

MELT THIS BOOK

It is not without some discomfort that I approach the grim business of "freezing" this mason jar of theatrical funk-fluid that was decidedly thawed, often bubbling, and always sweaty. *PS* was not a "property" you could skate through, unless you skated through sex, Holy-Ghost church services, crumbling relationships, revolution or the death of loved ones. To me it was a *Soul Train* dance through the primordial ooze-mess of life, and it never failed to both drown me (or was that baptizing?) and bring me back to life every night. Even our matinees were church.

Every single sentence of this ritual I gratefully sent through the filter of Annie Dorsen's take-no-prisoners mind, and she always handed them back to me with her invaluable adjustments, thoughts, suggestions, respectful demands, challenges, edits, arguments and laughter scribbled in the margins. Her contribution permeates every page of this play.

Heidi Rodewald not only wrote lots of beautiful music for this play but was also there from day one guiding me through the story and the characters, offering her strong, heartfelt opinions on the text and the vibe. We brought our love of '60s Los Angeles AM radio, '70s soul and OG punk rock to bear on the proceedings. And like any good musician, Heidi always tried to get us to remember how beautiful the silences were.

I'm not a playwright—as you are about to find out! I'm a songwriter. And actors are the coolest instruments to write for. Their sounds inspired these words.

Thanks to the band for providing the only context in which these words will ever make sense.

Next time I make an album, or any big life decision, I'm going to bring along a dramaturg. Mame Hunt and Madeleine Oldham went deep into this play at a time when I was far too scared to go there. Janice Paran said one sentence about *PS* back in 2004 that defined my entire approach to it for the next four years. Philip Himberg was *PS*'s #1 Soul Brother Superhero. And Oskar, thank you for reminding me that even the jokes have to be taken seriously.

This play was written in numerous cities and in a lot of kind people's homes. I cannot name you all. But the Wims of

Waltham, Mark Dolor of Hollyweird, Mara Manus, the Eder-Kaufmans of New York City and the good people at Tietzenweg 34, provided long stretches of shelter for me at pivotal moments when a place to concentrate was not easy to come by. Were it not for their hospitality and that of many unmentioned friends and family, this madness might have not made it from my brain to the page.

I'd like to thank Oskar Eustis, Tony Taccone, Les Waters, Rebecca Rugg, George Wolfe and of course Bill Bragin for hearing something in all this when there was nothing to hear in it, save for what it might sound like . . . someday.

Special thanks to my agent Bill Craver for guiding Heidi and me through the other "forest of sharp corners." Thanks also to Gerry Schoenfeld, Liz McCann, Joey Parnes and all our producers.

I'll never forget the 24 hours before our first rehearsal at the Sundance Theater Lab. Annie, Heidi and I sat around all day in a beautiful sun-drenched home, reading aloud, discussing and tearing apart the latest pages I'd written. But when night fell, those two escaped down to the Owl Bar, while I was ordered to stay home and write—for tomorrow would be our first day with real live actors. I wrote all night, drunk off my own cocktail of equal parts terror and excitement. The kid in *PS* experiences a lot of different drugs, but the one I got hooked on that morning at Sundance—watching the funk come together in the room in a swirl of words, music and movement charging madly and happily, like the rushing water right outside our rehearsal room door, towards some unknown revelation—changed my life forever. Since that morning on that strange mountain, I've been forever in search of that fix.

So be you a casual reader or someone actually crazy enough to wanna put this thing up, do me a favor and melt this play before using. Heat it up, let it become liquid and then imbibe it, inhale it, ingest it, inject it, let it run through your veins, your brain. Get stoned on this play.

We did.

—**Stew**

Cast and Credits

Passing Strange
Book and Lyrics by Stew
Music by Stew and Heidi Rodewald
Directed by and Created in Collaboration with Annie Dorsen

Passing Strange was originally produced in Berkeley, California, by the Berkeley Repertory Theatre, in New York by the Public Theater and at the Belasco Theater on Broadway by the Shubert Organization and others.

CAST IN ORDER OF APPEARANCE

NARRATOR	Stew
BASS / VOCALS	Heidi Rodewald
KEYBOARD / GUITAR / BACKING VOCALS	Jon Spurney
DRUMS	Christian Cassan
GUITAR / KEYBOARD / BACKING VOCALS	Christian Gibbs

Los Angeles

MOTHER	Eisa Davis
YOUTH	Daniel Breaker
TERRY, *a bad kid at church*	Chad Goodridge
SHERRY, *another bad kid at church*	Rebecca Naomi Jones
REVEREND JONES	Chad Goodridge
MR. FRANKLIN, *church pianist, youth choir director and the Reverend Jones' son*	Colman Domingo
MRS. KELSO	Rebecca Naomi Jones
EDWINA, *a teenage goddess*	de'Adre Aziza

Amsterdam

RENATA, *an abstract artist and café waitress*	Rebecca Naomi Jones
CHRISTOPHE, *an academic who moonlights*	Chad Goodridge
JOOP, *a body liberationist*	Colman Domingo
MARIANNA, *a neo-hippy*	de'Adre Aziza

Berlin

BORDER GUARD	Chad Goodridge
HUGO, *a militant music critic*	Chad Goodridge
SUDABEY, *an avant-garde filmmaker and writer*	de'Adre Aziza
DESI, *a den mother and social engineer*	Rebecca Naomi Jones
MR. VENUS, *a performance artist*	Colman Domingo

UNDERSTUDIES

For Mr. Franklin, Joop, Mr. Venus	Billy Eugene Jones
For Edwina, Marianna, Sudabey, Sherry, Renata, Desi	Kelly McCreary
For Mother	Karen Pittman
For Narrator	David Ryan Smith
For Youth, Hugo, Christophe, Terry	Lawrence Stallings

SCENIC DESIGN	David Korins
COSTUME DESIGN	Elizabeth Hope Clancy
LIGHTING DESIGN	Kevin Adams
SOUND DESIGN	Tom Morse
MUSIC SUPERVISION & ORCHESTRATIONS	Stew and Heidi Rodewald
MUSIC COORDINATOR	Seymour Red Press
CASTING	Jordan Thaler & Heidi Griffiths
PRODUCTION STAGE MANAGER	Tripp Phillips
PRESS REPRESENTATIVE	Sam Rudy Media Relations
COMPANY MANAGER	Kim Sellon
ASSOCIATE PRODUCER	S. D. Wagner
CHOREOGRAPHY	Karole Armitage
DANCE CAPTAIN	David Ryan Smith

Musical Numbers

Act One

Prologue ("We Might Play All Night")	Narrator, Heidi and the Band
"Baptist Fashion Show"	Narrator and Ensemble
"Church Blues Revelation"/ "Music Is the Freight Train in Which God Travels"	Narrator and Ensemble
"Arlington Hill"	Narrator
"Sole Brother"	Youth, Terry and Sherry
"Must Have Been High"	Narrator
"Mom Song"	Narrator, Mother and Ensemble
"Philistines"	Youth, Mother and Philistines
"Merci Beaucoup, M. Godard"	Narrator and Stewardesses
Headquarters Café Song: "Welcome to Amsterdam"	Ensemble
"Keys"	Marianna, Youth and Narrator
"We Just Had Sex"	Youth, Marianna and Renata
"Stoned"	Youth and Narrator

Act Two

"May Day"	Narrator and Ensemble
"Surface"	Mr. Venus
"Damage"	Narrator, Desi and Youth
"Identity"	Youth
"The Black One"	Narrator and Ensemble
"Come Down Now"	Heidi and Desi
"Youth's Unfinished Song"	Youth and Narrator
"Work the Wound"	Youth and Narrator
"Passing Phase"	Youth and Narrator
"Love Like That"	Narrator and Heidi

Act One

SONG: PROLOGUE
("WE MIGHT PLAY ALL NIGHT")

NARRATOR

Now you don't know me,
And I don't know you,
So let's cut to the chase,
The name is Stew.
And I'll be narrating this gig, so just sit tight,
We might play all night.

Been on the road, me, Heidi and this band
For ten thousand days of one-night stands,
And oh, by the way, can we crash on your couch tonight?
I said, "Is that alright? Is that alright?"

BAND

Is that alright?

NARRATOR

But before we cab it back to your uptown flat,
We're gonna do a little play since you paid for that.
A play where this band tells you where it's at,
So just follow along, just follow along.

BAND

Just follow along . . .

NARRATOR / HEIDI

Well, if this mic feeds back or the drums rock out,
Or an amp explodes or the bass player pouts,
Or if yer ever not sure what I'm on about,
Just ask the song.

BAND

Just ask the song . . .

NARRATOR / HEIDI

Just ask the song.

(MUSIC interlude. CAST enters.)

Los Angeles

NARRATOR *(Cont'd.)*
Now since it's my job, ah'ma set the scene,
In a big two-story, black middle-class dream.
With all the mod cons, the manicured lawns,
Some savings bonds, a Boy and his Mom . . .

BAND
A colored paradise where the palm trees sway,
A colored paradise where the palm trees sway . . .

NARRATOR
Cue music. Sunday morning. South Central L.A. 1976.
Mother stands in doorway. Youth is sleeping.

MOTHER
Wake up, pillow-huggin' son o' mine.
Iss yo turn ta rise 'n shine.
Fo' too long now you been on the wrong side of right,
I ain't studin' how late you was up lass night.

Lawd ham mercy, chile, look at cho head!
Look jus' like a feathuh bed!
Now let go dat pillow!
Leave dat dangerous dream be.
Jump outta dat bed 'n come a churchin' wit me!

NARRATOR
She drops the Negro dialect and speaks in her natural voice.

MOTHER
(Crisp middle-class tone.)

It's such a beautiful Sunday morning.

NARRATOR
And so begins her weekly sermon.

MOTHER
(Agitated but still with middle-class accent.)

Son, it wouldn't kill you to go to church this morning.

NARRATOR
Youth's eyes open.

MOTHER
And as for all this new Zen Buddha talk—

NARRATOR
Youth sits up in bed.

YOUTH

Zen Bu-ddhism!

MOTHER
The Bible clearly states, "Thou shalt place" or—wait a minute—how does it go again?

YOUTH / BAND
Ommmmmmmm.

MOTHER
I know you'd be happier in one of them white churches. Praising the lord in jeans and a T-shirt . . .

NARRATOR
She finds a jacket.

MOTHER
What about this one?

NARRATOR
She hurls it at him . . .

YOUTH
Four words, Mom: Brown. Poly. Ester. No.

MOTHER
Why are normal everyday things like sheer agony for you?

YOUTH

Cuz normal everyday things are phony. Why do I have to change?

YOUTH (*Cont'd.*) / BAND

Ommmmmmm.

MOTHER

Now look, Swami: the tiny inconvenience of a tie and a nice jacket *is a small price tuh pay fo' eternal life!*

NARRATOR

Note the return of the Negro dialect . . .

MOTHER

Since duh day they done dragged us offa dat slave ship, the church has been ah only real home!!!

NARRATOR

. . . rising to its authentic, authoritative crescendo!!!

MOTHER

Lawd only know what black folk woulda done without da church! Cuz there ain't nothin' in this ugly, unforgivin' world—and I mean nuthin'—like a good black church!

YOUTH

Then why don't you ever go?

SONG: "BAPTIST FASHION SHOW"

MOTHER

Those catty church bitches give me the blues,
And, Lord, look at these shoes . . .

NARRATOR

And you know . . .
Church people were all about the shoes.

BAND

Mama says you gotta go
To the Baptist Fashion Show . . .

NARRATOR

Silk ties, shiny purses, fancy hats and jewels.

BAND

Mama says you gotta go . . .
Jesus gonna save your soul . . .

NARRATOR

And that Christian catwalk was real unforgiving . . .

BAND

Mama says you gotta go,
But she didn't wanna go . . .

NARRATOR

. . . to anyone who couldn't fit in for a living.

BAND

Mama says you gotta go
To the Baptist Fashion Show . . .

MOTHER

Now, honestly, son, does this hat go with these shoes?

YOUTH

Colors are colors, Mom.

MOTHER

But if you had to choose?

YOUTH

If it was up to me . . .

MOTHER

You'd still be in bed, I know.

YOUTH

Why don't you go make some pancakes?

MOTHER

Then we'd be too late to go.

5

NARRATOR

war on Sunday morning . . .

YOUTH

I won't be breathing easy once this noose gets knotted . . .

NARRATOR

It was war on Sunday morning . . .

MOTHER

You men don't know how easy you got it.

NARRATOR

Now the church on Adams Boulevard is usually a bore.
The ladies wave fans and the old men snore.
The kids cut up on cue in the very back pew,
And the Holy Ghost ain't been here since 1972.

PHILISTINES

Look who's here, seems like we never see you anymore!

NARRATOR

They got real estate, college funds, jobs with benefits,
Home-owners, debutantes . . .

YOUTH

This place is as phony as it gets.

NARRATOR

LOOK! Everybody sharp,
Ain't not one head nappy.
But it's been a long time since this church got happy.
With their judgmental eyes,
See, they've all just realized . . .

PHILISTINES

(At YOUTH.*)*

Fourteen years old and *still* ain't been baptized . . .

MOTHER

Son, bring me a fan and a tithing envelope.

YOUTH

Like they ain't got enough money already . . .

NARRATOR

Now just as he thought, "This'll be a nightmare come true,"
His conviction turned to ice in that chilly church pew,
His conviction turned to ice in that chilly church pew.

(MUSIC *stops abruptly.*)

YOUTH

Jesus'll make it back here before I do.

NARRATOR

He saw the brownskin-ded ladies in their oversized crowns,
And the jet-black deacons with those "Don't you do that" frowns,
And those high yellow girls in their skin-tight gowns,
A collection of verbs disguised as nouns.

And ev'ry Sunday she pushed him,
But she never wanted to go.
Ev'ry Sunday he listened,
But he didn't want to know.

It's too bad they never talked about,
The shared truth that dwelled below:
Who could handle the pressure
Of this Baptist Fashion Show?

(Chord, then MUSIC *segues.*)

SONG: "CHURCH BLUES REVELATION"

HEIDI

Listening is waiting . . .
Listening is waiting . . .

NARRATOR	**HEIDI** (*Cont'd.*) **/ CHORUS**
(*Speaking over* CHORUS.)	(*Under* NARRATOR.)

The whole congregation was
listening and waiting   *Listening is waiting . . .*
To be released from its collective frown.
Even the bad kids in the back
pew were wondering . . .   *Listening is waiting . . .*

SHERRY / TERRY
Is something real gonna go down?

NARRATOR	**HEIDI / CHORUS**

Now some said: "Lord,
please read us,   *Listening is waiting . . .*
Collect us, then lead us
to higher ground."
And then all asked the
very same question . . .   *Listening is waiting . . .*

CHORUS (*Cont'd.*)
Is somethin' real goin' . . . down, down, down?

(MUSIC *stops, sustaining on the word "real."*)

MOTHER
Lord . . . show up and save him this morning.

(MUSIC *begins, quiet rumble.*)

Show him you are real.

NARRATOR
And then the chilly church pews got suddenly warm,
And the notes of the music began to swarm,
And then bridges of spirit began to form,
Subjecting and connecting everyone
To what they needed to feel . . .
This is how a church made way for the real.

Waiting and vibrating for more than Christ's sake,
As the organ started doing that earthquake shake
Where it sounds like the speakers are starting to break.

And time itself slipped into earth's crack,
And Mrs. Kelso's getting happy,
And she keeps hitting you on the back.
And Mr. Franklin played piano like he was mad at it,
Till it started to hum,
And the church was gettin' bad at it.
Like a stained glass drum,
Like a stained glass drum,
Like a stained glass drum.
And the mystery of life was
On it's way to gettin' solved.
Don't look now, church,
I think the Real's gettin' involved.

(MUSIC *stops.*)

And then something strange happened. Something that's never happened in this church . . .

YOUTH

I'm having a religious experience!

MOTHER

Thank you, Jesus!

YOUTH

This is real!!

MOTHER

Thank you, Lord!

YOUTH

It's mighty real!!

MOTHER

Reel him in, Heavenly Father!

YOUTH

'Scuse me while I kiss the sky!!

9

NARRATOR

And then the right Reverend Jones revved up and started banging the pulpit like a conga drum and his screams cut through the organ's swell like a bolt of sonic lightning and then it struck.

YOUTH

Oh, FUCK!

REVEREND JONES

Ahm uh tell y'all a story 'bout Apostle Paul.

(*NARRATOR's Guitar mimics* JONES.)

YOUTH

Could you repeat that?

REVEREND JONES

I said: *Ahm uh tell y'all a story 'bout Apostle Paul.*

(*BASS and Guitar mimic* JONES.)

NARRATOR

Cruisin' up and down that fretboard like it was the road to Damascus.

REVEREND JONES

Where you headed, Pilgrim?

NARRATOR

If you don't know the way, you better ask us.

REVEREND JONES

You better ask somebody!

NARRATOR

IT WAS A MIND!

CHORUS

Yeah!!!

NARRATOR

EXPANDING!!!

CHORUS

Yeah!!!

NARRATOR

REVELATION!!!

CHORUS

Yeah!!!

NARRATOR

REVELATION . . .

CHORUS

Yeah!!!

NARRATOR

REVELATION!!!

CHORUS

Yeah, yeah, yeaaahhhhhh!!!

(*REVEREND does his Holy Ghost, rock star preacher thang.*)

REVEREND JONES
(Over MUSIC and ad libs.)

Who came here to feel the spirit?
Who came here to get inspired?
We built this house on love.
Can you feel it?

NARRATOR
Yeah, the boy and the Reverend are tradin' licks now,
Gettin' hotter than a party on the River Styx now.
Leading the church on a Holy Ghost search,
It's a pilgrimage of a solo,
It's a Fillmore West Bank solo.
Yer tappin' ya foot, but you don't hear me, though.

And the boy is tagging along,
Behind the message in his song,
He was freed, guaranteed,

Had to let the pilgrim lead.
Come on, Rev!

REVEREND JONES

Now is God real?

CHOIR

Oh yes, he's real . . .

REVEREND JONES

Well, can you deal with the real?

CHOIR

We can deal with the Real.

REVEREND JONES

Now is God real?

CHOIR

Oh yes, he's real . . .

REVEREND JONES

Well, can you deal with the real?

CHOIR

We can deal with the Real.

REVEREND JONES

Now is God real?

CHOIR

Oh yes, he's real . . .

REVEREND JONES

Well, can you deal with the real?

CHOIR

We can deal with the Real.

REVEREND JONES

Hit me with the Holy Ghost!!!

NARRATOR
The bubble was expanding . . . there was a new understanding.

SONG: "MUSIC IS THE FREIGHT TRAIN IN WHICH GOD TRAVELS"

(REVEREND JONES baptizes YOUTH as MOTHER assists.)

NARRATOR / REVEREND JONES / YOUTH
Music is the freight train in which God travels,
Bang! It does its thang and then my soul unravels.
Heals like holy water and it fights all my battles,
Music is the freight train in which God travels.

REVEREND JONES / MOTHER
Music is the freight train in which God travels,
Bang! It does its thang and then my soul unravels.
Heals like holy water and it fights all my battles,
Music is the freight train in which God travels.

(Church piano and organ fall away, revealing a percussion-based rhythm, which overtakes the congregation, including YOUTH and MOTHER, and finds them dancing in a style most African indeed . . .)

YOUTH	REV. JONES / CHOIR *(Under.)*
Mom, I can feel the spirit and it's real! Check it out: Reverend Jones is singing the blues!	*Now is God real?* *Yes, he's real . . .* *Well, can you deal with the real?*
And what we're doing is call and response— we brought it over from the motherland! Mom, we're all just a tribe of bluesy Africans and church ain't nothin' but rock and roll . . .	*We can deal with the Real . . .* *Now is God real? Yes, he's real . . .* *Well, can you deal with the real?* *We can deal with the Real . . .* *Now is God real?*

(MOTHER slaps YOUTH as music abruptly stops.)

YOUTH

But it was on PBS.

MOTHER

Are you trying to embarrass me in front of all these people?

YOUTH

But that was the coolest thing that's ever happened here.

MOTHER

Do you want these people thinking I've raised a heathen?

YOUTH

I'm not like you! I don't care what they think.

MOTHER

Don't you know the difference between the sacred and the profane?

YOUTH

I can't hear the difference.

NARRATOR

She slapped him back into himself,
And then he pulled away,
To be nurtured by his destiny
On that warm L.A. Sunday.

And so it was in church he began his search
Down a road that would not bend.
In stained glass light the pilgrim went in search
Of a song that would not end.

YOUTH

(*Muttered to himself.*)

I gotta get outta these clothes . . .

NARRATOR

And there he goes . . .

YOUTH

(Disdainful.)

After service, Mom and I are church ce-le-bri-ties.

ALL

Praise Jesus.

MOTHER

(Nervous.)

Flash bulb smiles—light us up—like pa-pa-raz-zi.

ALL

Praise God.

YOUTH

A Christian Kodak Moment is what air-body want.

ALL

That's right!

YOUTH / MOTHER

Now we are a Ma-don-na and Child ta-bleau vi-vant.

ALL

Smile, God damn it!

NARRATOR

Enter Mr. Franklin, the Reverend's piano-banging son.

MR. FRANKLIN

How are you, Miss Irma? *Tu va bien?*

(MOTHER seeks refuge in MR. FRANKLIN.)

MOTHER

Oui. Franklin, you are SO talented! I just love the way you spice up those old spirituals!

(Conspiratorial whisper.)

And I don't care what these old fogeys think! "Onward, Christian Soldiers" as a rhumba? You go 'head on, boy!

(BOTH *laugh.*)

MR. FRANKLIN
Oh, I'm so glad you liked the arrangement!

(*Facetiously.*)

It's God's work, you know. I'm just the vessel.

(*Under his breath, teasing.*)

And, girl, you lookin' so Marilyn McCoo today, you must be tryin' to catch one!

MOTHER
Franklin, you know I look terrible. If I had the nerve, one day I'd show up here in an outrageous gown and show everyone.

MR. FRANKLIN
You go 'head on, girl!

YOUTH
(*Mockingly limp-wristed.*)

You go 'head on, girl . . .

MOTHER
If it's the last thing I do, I'm gonna get him into your choir.

YOUTH
THAT . . . is not going to happen!

MR. FRANKLIN
Choir is a fabulous place to develop one's harmonic sensibilities!

YOUTH
I'm developing my own *sthensthibilities.*

MRS. KELSO
Did I hear you say yer joining the youth choir?

YOUTH

No, I'm not. See what none of you understand is that—

(Enter EDWINA.)

EDWINA

So yer joining the youth choir! Lord knows we could use a new . . .

(Eyes his crotch.)

. . . member.

NARRATOR

Ever since her transformation into a teenage goddess, Edwina Williams never said more to him than:

EDWINA

(Nonchalant.)

"Hey."

NARRATOR

In that half-hearted way teenage goddesses are obliged to do. Oh, but now her magnetic eyes were fixed on him, drawing him into the vortex of her Ebony *magazine smile.*

EDWINA

Heyyyyy!!!!!!!!

NARRATOR

Oh-oh, Sunday morning's steamy stained glass window vision . . .

EDWINA

I am the way . . .

NARRATOR

. . . the wriggling bait at the end of God's fishing hook . . .

EDWINA

I am the truth . . .

NARRATOR

She was the Master's Bait . . .

EDWINA

. . . and the light . . .

NARRATOR

She was a Prayboy Bunny, Lord . . .

EDWINA

Airbrushed by the almighty.

NARRATOR / YOUTH

Whooo!!

EDWINA

You in *my* choir now!

YOUTH

Ohhhhhhh, laaaawwwd ham-mercy!!!!

(A low, ominous gospel piano rumble begins.)

EDWINA

You want some uh this blessing?

YOUTH

Yes, brown sugar!!!

EDWINA

I said: Do you want some uh this blessing?

YOUTH

Yes, brown sugar!!!

EDWINA

Then I need some new clothes.

YOUTH

Yes, brown sugar!!!

EDWINA

You gotta do something about your hair.

YOUTH

Yes, brown sugar!!!

EDWINA

And get that B.A. in Communications from a prestigious black college.

YOUTH

Yes, brown sugar!!!

EDWINA

And after we marry and you've got a job in the corporate sector, you'll buy me a sprawling two-story house fulla African sculptures from tribes we know nothing about, kente cloth couch covers, and Malcolm X commemorative plates lining the walls of our airy, peach-colored breakfast nook!!!

YOUTH

Yes, brown sug . . .

(MUSIC *stops.*)

—uh, breakfast nook?

EDWINA

And lastly, you'll need to blacken up a bit.

YOUTH

Blacken up?

EDWINA

Yeah. Like not so much that you become un-hirable or anything, but you know, you kinda act too white. You're not black enough for me!!! Put a little soul in your stroll.

NARRATOR

Had he assumed the costume he could have bathed in her fire. But he's still gotta deal with that dorky youth choir . . .

Mr. Franklin's Prayer Circle.
Volkswagen Bug.

TERRY

Greetings, Christian comrade. Mr. Franklin has requested your presence.

SHERRY

At the prayer circle.

YOUTH

What?

TERRY

It's a mandatory ritual for new choir members.

YOUTH

Oh, God.

SHERRY

Exactly!

MR. FRANKLIN

Welcome to the prayer circle!

NARRATOR

He smoked his first joint that Thursday afternoon—right before choir rehearsal—in a powder blue VW bug parked atop Arlington Hill, overlooking South Central L.A. The man behind the wheel was none other than Franklin Jones.

MR. FRANKLIN

I'm just the vessel.

NARRATOR

Church pianist, youth choir director, but, more significantly, the Reverend Jones' son.

YOUTH

That's right, Mom! I'm smoking weed with the Reverend's son!

(Referring to joint.)

He works in mysterious ways indeed!

(ALL *laugh*.)

NARRATOR

Our hero had found his tribe. Now Sherry and Terry were the bad kids at church. Terry obsessively drew cartoons of Jesus . . . *water-skiing.*

TERRY

Check it out!

NARRATOR

And Sherry always looked at our hero as if she knew his most carefully guarded secret. And as for Mr. Franklin, well, he was a completely different person when it wasn't *Sunday morning.*

MR. FRANKLIN
(Imitating soprano opera singin'.)

"Vissi d'arte" . . . "Hello . . . Maria Callas speaking . . . Yes, it's me, darlings, with my funny nose, skinny legs and all. And I have nothing to hide . . . If I were any more real . . . child, I'd be fictional! . . . Children, if we were in Amsterdam right now, we'd be inhaling this . . . this sacrament . . . in a comfy café with a wicked cup of espresso . . ."

TERRY / SHERRY / YOUTH

In public?

MR. FRANKLIN

In flagrante delicto, kinder! Nobody's . . . hiding anything over there, dig me?

YOUTH

WOW.

SONG: "ARLINGTON HILL"

NARRATOR

He took a hit for the first time
In a bug on Arlington Hill.

Hip to hip, shoulder to shoulder,
The radio, it blasts in everyone's ear.
Oh, she sees you there in the rear view,
Choking on smoke and trying to be cool.

When he and Mr. Franklin were parked up there on Arlington Hill, just the two of them . . . it was like sitting next to a soulfully played cello. Franklin made him feel like that powder blue VW bug was just hovering over South Central and y'all were just escaped slaves "in a beautiful balloon" and yes, there's a place in this world . . .

MR. FRANKLIN

. . . for whatever—

NARRATOR

. . . for everyone . . .

MR. FRANKLIN

. . . and whoever you are tonight! I mean, baby, we're all freaks depending on the backdrop, yenno?

YOUTH

(Giggly, stoned.)

Heh heh . . . Yeah.

(Brief pause.)

We're *ALL* freaks . . .

MR. FRANKLIN

(Stoned but serious.)

. . . lookin' for a home. And as for this philistine fish bowl we're swimmin' around in? Shoot! If you wanna deal with Le Real, I'm talking Stockholm, baby, "Persona," yenno? I'm talking 'bout Rome and one of them "La Dolce Vita" parties, yenno? I'm talking 'bout Godard's Paris, baby, I mean cuz we a "Band of Outsiders" too, yenno? I mean I'm talking 'bout brother Al Camus . . . "The Stranger." Brother said, "Algeria? See ya! Wouldn't wanna be ya!" OK? I'm talkin' little Jimmy Baldwin, baby—you gotta go to Another Country if you wanna get to Giovanni's Room! HA! That's what I'm talking 'bout!

NARRATOR

Half the time he didn't know what the fuck Mr. Franklin was talking about. But that was cool cuz Franklin's words would just wash over him like a Bach fugue creeping out of a cheap car stereo, on the brother side of midnight. You know how when the music goes right over your head and straight into that part of you which is most beautiful? I mean when your mind can't grasp the music's math and your heartbeat has no clue, your pilgrim soul just follows the melody's path, looks back and says I wanna thank you, brother . . . thank you for this fugue. And it just is and is and is and is so much that whether you get it or not—it's got.

MR. FRANKLIN

La Baker walking a panther down the boulevard . . .

NARRATOR

Oh-oh, Adams and Crenshaw is beautiful
And they are laughing in the sun.
Then they parachute into church
So they can sing before practice is done.
When they raise one voice:

CHORUS

Ahhhhhhhhh . . .

NARRATOR

Stoned angels weep,
Then he feels the Holy Ghost
Creeping up slowly . . .

YOUTH

Where should I go in Europe?

MR. FRANKLIN

Anywhere.

YOUTH

Where did you go?

MR. FRANKLIN

Nowhere. Holy Father keeps me on a short leash . . . keeps me in check by . . . signing the checks. You could say he's paying me to . . . not be myself. I'd like to say I'm chained to the church piano. But that would an insult to . . . actual slaves . . .

NARRATOR

These were the parameters of the cage.

MR. FRANKLIN

Because you see, my boy, hmph . . . slaves . . . ha ha ha . . . SLAVES! YES, that's it!! Slaves got options! Options, ya dig? I'm talking escape . . . revolt . . . death.

(Pause.)

Options.

(Pause.)

But cowards ain't got shit! Cowards only have . . . consequences.

(Silence.)

Dig me?

(Silence.)

Do you dig me?

NARRATOR

Hey, man, don't let him know yer freaked out . . . Say something clever.

YOUTH

I don't believe in God.

MR. FRANKLIN

Does he know?

(Pause.)

I appreciate your feeling compelled to share one of your deep and dirty secrets with me. That was very sweet of you. I apologize if I went overboard.

(Pause.)

So, in this corner, the sensitive, artistic soul . . . and in this corner, moi, La Franklin . . . the wicked Baptist rebel. Yet in the end we're just two brothers . . .

(Thinks for a sec or two.)

. . . passing.

(This epiphany hits him hard . . . Mr. Franklin is perhaps growing a bit angry now.)

Like your high yellow grandma back in the day, only we're passing for black folks. Good, lawn trimmin', tax payin', morally upstanding, narrow-minded Christian black folk! Now ain't that a bitch?

YOUTH
(Eureka.)

Black folks passing for black folks. That's a trip!

MR. FRANKLIN
If it were any more real, baby—

YOUTH
(Practically ignoring MR. FRANKLIN—still lost in his eureka moment.)

It'd be fiction . . .

MR. FRANKLIN
(Slightly taken aback at the change in YOUTH.)

Well, holler . . .

NARRATOR
And suddenly there is meaning.

Arlington Hill helped him see everything.
Yeah, suddenly there is meaning.
And everything's all right,
Everything's all right.

NARRATOR (*Cont'd.*) / MR. FRANKLIN
Everything's all right,
Everything's all right.

NARRATOR (*Cont'd.*) / BAND / ALL BUT YOUTH
Everything's all right.
Everything's all right.
Everything's all right.
Everything's all right.
Everything's all right.
Everything's all right . . .

NARRATOR
Find a garage with a lot of space.
Get Sherry to buy a little pawnshop bass.
And if Terry can't play, just make him understand—
It ain't no problem . . .
This is punk rock, man!

(We come in on the last long chord of a punk song . . .
electric atonal cacophony. YOUTH, SHERRY and TERRY in a
rehearsal studio.)

TERRY
I suck! I suck! I suck! I told you I couldn't play drums.

SHERRY
And we should've believed you!

YOUTH
Look, it's not about playing the right notes . . . it's about pure
energy and relentless self-expression!

TERRY
My dad says the odds of making it in the music biz are zero.

YOUTH
So go sell air conditioners like him . . .

SHERRY

(To TERRY.)

Yeah, just forget about our music career.

TERRY

We have no music career—we suck!

YOUTH

I'd rather suck at this than be great at selling air conditioners. Do you think yer Dad's happy?

(TERRY and YOUTH have a moment.)

SHERRY

Can we play the fucking song?

YOUTH

(To TERRY.)

Go ask him.

(Adopts punky stage pose.)

Ladies and Jerks! We are . . .

NARRATOR

THE SCARYOTYPES!!!

SONG: "SOLE BROTHER"

YOUTH

1-2-3-4,
1-2-3-4.
I'm at war with Negro mores.
I'm at war with ghetto norms.
My mother stands in doorways beggin' me to conform.
Be a good football-playin', snazzy-dressin' brother,
So the sisters won't be able to tell me from the others . . .

Yeah, I'm the sole brother—up in this motherfucker.

Yeah, I'm the sole brother—up in this motherfucker.
Yeah, I'm the sole brother—up in this motherfucker.
Yeah, I'm the soul brother here.

So Roots blew your mind? You didn't know it was that bad?
I learned that shit in third grade. In Miss Medearis' class.
But yer still a buncha slaves. And yer driving me insane.
Cuz the whip across your shoulder is connected to your brain . . .

(YOUTH *and* SHERRY *lock eyes in excited yet dead serious recognition of the fact that this song is kicking ass.*)

MOTHER

There are some sandwiches in the den, for when you kids get hungry.

YOUTH

MOM!
1-2-3-4,
1-2-3-4.
I'm the sole brother.

SHERRY

And it's not alright-tuh!!!

YOUTH

I'm the sole brother!!!

SHERRY

And it's not alright-tuh!!!

YOUTH

I'm the sole brother!!!

SHERRY

And it's not alright-tuh!!!

YOUTH / SHERRY

I'm / he's the soul brother here!!!

(*Song ends.* BAND *applauds. Enter* MR. FRANKLIN.)

TERRY

Man, that was the best it ever sounded! We're gonna be huge!

MR. FRANKLIN

Bravo, children, bravissimo. Listen—my father just informed me he's giving the youth choir a Sunday all to ourselves! So look, this is gonna take lots of rehearsal and—

YOUTH

We're rehearsing *now*, man.

MR. FRANKLIN

Mon frere, is it time for a little lesson in priorities?

YOUTH

Yeah, I guess it is.

SHERRY

(*Trying to lighten the tense vibe.*)

Franklin, man . . . us . . .

(*Refers to* BAND.)

. . . and the choir . . . it ain't workin' for us no more . . .

MR. FRANKLIN

What "ain't workin'"?

YOUTH

The double life shit ain't workin' . . .

SHERRY

Wait.

MR. FRANKLIN

Double life?

SHERRY

What he means is—

YOUTH

The band is our choir now.

(Slight pause.)

We're writing our own songs.

MR. FRANKLIN

Songs? So that's what you're calling them.

YOUTH

Spicing up the spirituals with your stupid ass little arrangements ain't got shit to do with . . .

(Mocking.)

. . . dealing with "Le Real." You see, we're gonna live . . . the way you . . . just talk. We're not in your little car anymore.

TERRY

Hey, Franklin, man. We're rehearsing.

*(*MUSIC *starts.)*

Acid Trip

NARRATOR

The punk rock freight train turned with the tide
Into a psychedelic, underground railroad ride . . .

TERRY

(Passing out tabs.)

Lucy in the Sky with Diamonds, man . . . My brother says this shit is wicked . . . Hold on to your hats . . .

(As THEY *all look to each other hesitantly to see who will drop first . . .)*

YOUTH

Welcome to the New School of Slave Rebellion.

*(*YOUTH *drops.)*

SONG: "MUST HAVE BEEN HIGH"

NARRATOR

See Terry's folks, they'd gone out of town,
So they bought a sheet and they all got down.
Chandelier eyes and electric chairs,
Visit your mind and spend two days there.

Where every song sounds just like an angels' choir.
Your edges get rounded, you'll have wings of fire.
Soaring through the sky
They must have been—

(BAND INSTRUMENTAL.)

SHERRY

We gotta tour, man. I can't wait to tour the country.

YOUTH

Fuck this fishbowl. If we're gonna deal with the real, we gotta tour Europe. Hendrix had to go there to get famous. America can't handle freaky Negroes.

SHERRY

We gotta start saving money to get over there.

TERRY

We're not going anywhere.

YOUTH

What?

SHERRY

Shut up!

TERRY

We're tripping now . . . but when this trip is over . . . we're still gonna be right here, just north of the 10 Freeway between Crenshaw Boulevard and West Boulevard on 4257 Saturn Saturn Saturn Saturn Drive! And you wanna know whhhhhhhhy, MAN!!!???? Cuz we're not going ANYWHERE!!!

YOUTH

That's bullshit, man!

TERRY

Is not! It's been two years and I still can't find my natural sense of rhythm!

SHERRY

(To YOUTH.)

Make him stop . . .

TERRY

Look at Franklin! He never made it out. You really think yer better than him? DO YOU??

YOUTH

Look, man, it's not about who's better than—

TERRY

We're all gonna wake up one day and be thirty years old, man!

(SHERRY screams.)

YOUTH

Why you gotta get all morbid and shit, man?

TERRY

Oh, God . . . it's happening right now . . . look . . . I'm aging . . . I'm aging . . . my skin is wrinkling . . .

YOUTH

Yer just high, man.

TERRY

That's no excuse! (Pause.) I've just turned thirty.

(Big crash from the BAND.)

I'm thirty and my life is over. And I haven't even been to Sea World. But that's OK cuz I'll just go there with my boring wife . . . who hates music . . . and my ugly kids . . . who hate me! Help me, somebody! I'm a resident of Los Angeles! I know what it's like to be dead!!!

(*MUSIC out.*)

YOUTH
(*Shaken but trying to appear in control.*)

Well . . . we'll just have to get another drummer!

SHERRY
We're a band! How can you say that?

YOUTH
We can't make it unless we make the band our life. And he's scared.

SHERRY
So what if I get scared . . . you gonna kick me out too?

(*Pause. YOUTH does not answer but his silence does.*)

NARRATOR
And everything mattered,
It's so different now.
The ashes were scattered,
They moved on somehow
Never asking why,
They must have been high.
They must have been high.

Sitting on the balcony watching the rail rust,
Time slips through your fingers . . .

HEIDI
Slips through your fingers just like angel dust,
Slips through your fingers just like angel dust,
Slips through your fingers just like angel dust,
Slips through your fingers just like angel dust . . .

SONG: "MOM SONG"

NARRATOR

It's breaking your heart,
His questioning of everything.
Unannounced, he's flown
Out from under your wing.

MOTHER

I'm hardly afraid
Of your new world's strange design.
Why don't you make room for me,
As I made room for you in mine?

See, I've been running from this world
For far longer than you.
But I didn't know where else to go,
So I hid from it in you.
And then, for a time,
This world was yours and mine,
And that was only yesterday, you see,
But now you've got your own thing
And it does not include me.

NARRATOR

It's breaking her heart.
She says you seem so distant these days.

MOTHER

Unannounced you've grown
Into a living thing . . .

NARRATOR

Into a living thing . . .

MOTHER

Into a living thing . . .

NARRATOR

Into a living thing . . .

SONG: "PHILISTINES"

PHILISTINES

There he is!

UNCLE #1

How nice of Mr. Musician to grace us with his presence.

AUNT #1

Seems like we never see you anymore.

UNCLE #2

You still messin' around with that guitar?

AUNT #2

Terry and Sherry gave up that mess a long time ago.

AUNTS 1 & 2

Unh, unh, unh . . .

PHILISTINES

Instead of trying to find yourself, why don't you try to find a job?

UNCLE #2

"I'm just tryin' ta' live mah life"??? You better leave that kinda crap to whitey!

YOUTH

Gotta get away from these philistines, philistines!!!

PHILISTINES	MOTHER
(Overlapping.)	*(Overlapping.)*
This is your life and it's the only one you've got, This is your life and there ain't no way out!!!	*Make room for me, As I made room for you.*
This is your life and it's the only one you've got, This is your life and there ain't no way out!!!	*Make room for me, As I made room for you.*

(MUSIC *stops.*)

YOUTH

Ain't no way out, huh? Is that what you think? Well, guess what! You know what I'm saving money for? I'm going to Europe. And not just to visit. I'm moving there for good!

NARRATOR

At this point in the play we were planning a show tune!
An upbeat "gotta leave this town" kinda show tune!
But we don't know how to write those kinds of tunes . . .

However, we do know how to make fun of European avant garde cinema. So without further ado . . .

(*Lights up on* YOUTH *and* MOTHER. *They are in a black and white Antonioni movie.* MUSIC *under.*)

YOUTH

I have my ticket . . .

MOTHER

Such a selfish person I never dreamed I'd raise. And how callously you serve me my fate . . . to die alone . . . in this shell of a house.

YOUTH

This brings me no joy.

MOTHER

Joy is for children.

YOUTH

Then I remain a child.

MOTHER

What is wrong with a comfortable home, a loving family and sunshine all year round?

YOUTH

All of the above.

MOTHER

People died so that you might enjoy these comforts.

YOUTH

And those comforts are killing me.

MOTHER

How can you be so unappreciative?

YOUTH

It's easy. My dream is to live as an artist.

MOTHER

Love is more real than a dream.

YOUTH

What would you know about dreams?

MOTHER

That they can haunt you . . . to your grave. That they can be . . . torture.

YOUTH

You torture me with love when what I need is understanding.

MOTHER

You formed inside my body. I understand everything about you.

YOUTH

You understand nothing! Clearly you've never had a dream!!!

(MOTHER *takes off Euro-garb and Euro-persona and stares daggers at* YOUTH.)

MOTHER

(Really pissed.)

Is that what you think?

YOUTH

. . . not a dream like mine . . . not a dream like this . . .

MOTHER

I am at least owed an explanation for why you are destroying my life.

NARRATOR

Well, it's something like this—

SONG: "MERCI BEAUCOUP, M. GODARD"

STEWARDESSES	NARRATOR
La la la la la la la la la la	
La la la la la la la la la la	
La la la la la la la la la la	
La la la la la la la la la la.	
La la la la la la la la la la,	*Naked girls at breakfast tables*
La la la la la la la la la la.	*Talking Hegel and Camus.*

YOUTH

Adieu, Disneyland!

STEWARDESSES	NARRATOR
La la la la la la la la la la,	*While men dressed up in*
	Gauloise smoke
La la la la la la la la la la.	*Quote Marx right back at you.*

YOUTH

Auf wiedersehen, L.A.P.D.!

STEWARDESSES	NARRATOR
La la la la la la la la la la,	*All this might seem obscure,*
La la la la la la la la la la.	*That would depend on who*
	you are.

YOUTH

Ciao, ciao, Mr. Ray-gun!

STEWARDESSES	NARRATOR
La la la la la la la la la la,	*Fellini, Truffaut, Pasolini,*
La la la la la la la la!	*And don't forget Monsieur*
	Godard.

NARRATOR
Can you dig it?

STEWARDESS ONE
Welcome aboard Air Amsterdam Flight Zero.

NARRATOR
A panorama of sculpture!
Of music, painting and culture!

STEWARDESS TWO
Non-stop to the Real . . .

NARRATOR
An intellectual arcade.
Did I say he needed to get laid?

(BAND *makes sound of airplane taking off.*)

Amsterdam

HEADQUARTERS CAFÉ SONG: "WELCOME TO AMSTERDAM"

BAND
Amsterdam, spring sunshine . . .
Amsterdam, spring sunshine . . .

NARRATOR
So now let's jet the scene of the crime,
Touch down in once upon a time.
As Plasticland gives way
To a new world born today.

Amsterdam, spring sunshine,
And the vibe is alive and the girls look fine.
He sits in a café, like Baldwin in the day.

Day-glo walls, incense air,
Lounging 'round in velvet chairs.
So glad he took the trip
Out the slave-holder's grip.

He knew his destiny was looming,
And an epiphany was blooming,
And the lost was gonna get profound,
And the real was about to go down.

And he saw that his whole journey through the bowels of the middle-class coon show had led him to this single moment of utter crystalline clarity, for the Real was to be revealed right here within this very venue!!!

YOUTH

There's hashish on the menu!!!

CHORUS

Ahhh!

YOUTH	**CHORUS** (*Cont'd.*)
(*Overlapping.*)	(*Under.*)
. . . and prostitutes in windows . . .	*Ahhh!*
All vices in full view . . .	*Ahhh!*

NARRATOR

Everything was in its proper place,
Including the smile on his face.

(*The Headquarters Café* PATRONS *reveal themselves.*
RENATA *working the bar while leisurely sketching him*
breaks his reverie.)

RENATA

Like another coffee while you make up your mind?

YOUTH

Thank you, yes, excuse me, I'm still startled by the sign.

CHRISTOPHE

This one's free, man, it's on me, you don't have to pay.

RENATA

How'z about a sample of the special of the day?
This your first time?

YOUTH

Does it show? I'm like an ice cube gone to melt.

RENATA

I hope you find yourself at home.

YOUTH

I like the cards that I've been dealt.

JOOP

And how's your mind?

YOUTH

Oh, it's blown . . . it's a vibe I've never felt.

RENATA

Welcome to Amsterdam! Amsterdam!
I'm your flight attendant, Miss Renata Holiday.
Welcome to Amsterdam! Amsterdam!
And I welcome you most happily to our little café . . .

YOUTH

No way!

RENATA

I make abstract drawings because representational art is just an ego stroke, you know?

CHRISTOPHE

I'm Christophe. I'm a Philosophy professor and part-time sex worker. You could say, I hook, therefore I . . .

CHORUS / BAND

Amsterdam . . . Amsterdam . . .

JOOP

My name is Joop and I believe everyone should be naked all the time. Clothes are chains from which we must break free! I'm naked therefore I . . .

CHORUS / BAND

Amsterdam . . . Amsterdam . . .

MARIANNA

I'm Marianna. And I'm into tantric meditation, organic psychedelics and white magic.

YOUTH

White magic . . . wow.

MARIANNA

And anything that's beyond my understanding . . .

YOUTH

Uh . . . white magic, wow.

MARIANNA

It might sound strange . . . but that's just who I . . .

CHORUS / BAND

Amsterdam . . . Amsterdam . . .

JOOP

The enlightened aren't frightened,
We let untamed spirits roam.

CHORUS / BAND

Only in Amsterdam . . . Amsterdam . . .

CHRISTOPHE

But we're the freedom experts, man,
So don't try this at home!

CHORUS / BAND

Only in Amsterdam . . . Amsterdam . . .

RENATA

While there ain't no witch or a yellow brick road . . .

MARIANNA

It's an emerald city after two bong loads of . . .

CHORUS / BAND

Amsterdam . . . Amsterdam . . .

"And I was like, 'Damn, pretzel man.'"
Stew

"An intellectual arcade. Did I say he needed to get laid?"
Left to right: Rebecca Naomi Jones, Stew and de'Adre Aziza

Heidi Rodewald

"What's inside is just a lie."
Colman Domingo, foreground, and Daniel Breaker

"Amsterdam, spring sunshine, and the vibe is alive and the girls look fine."
Left to right: Daniel Breaker, Chad Goodridge and Rebecca Naomi Jones

"If I were any more real . . . child, I'd be fictional!"

Left to right: Daniel Breaker, Rebecca Naomi Jones,
Colman Domingo and Chad Goodridge

The Negro Problem, AKA the *Passing Strange* band, in front of Broadway's Belasco Theater, from left to right: Christian Cassan, Jon Spurney, Heidi Rodewald and Christian Gibbs

"Have a discussion with ze hand!"
Stew, left, and Rebecca Naomi Jones

"I am the way . . . I am the truth . . . and the light . . ."
Eisa Davis, left, and de'Adre Aziza

"There's hashish on the menu!!!"

Daniel Breaker

"Can you deal with the real?"
Left to right: Chad Goodridge, Daniel Breaker, Stew and Eisa Davis

"I dun' broke my chains and escaped to the North!"
Daniel Breaker, foreground

"Lord . . . show up and save him this morning."
Left to right: Daniel Breaker, Stew and Eisa Davis

"May Day, May Day, there's a riot going down, in a deep, dark corner of West Berlin town!"

Left to right: Rebecca Naomi Jones, Christian Gibbs (bottom), Stew, Chad Goodridge, Daniel Breaker and Colman Domingo

"Now . . . I need something more than real."
Stew, left, and Daniel Breaker

"So now let's jet the scene of the crime, touch down in once upon a time."
Stew

CHRISTOPHE

You can trip all day till your mind just melts.

JOOP

Makes Berkeley look like the Bible Belt!

CHORUS / BAND

Amsterdam . . . Amsterdam . . . WHOO!

(PATRONS *baptize him in their human river.*)

NARRATOR

*The Pilgrim made some progress and was pleased he'd gone
forth . . .*

YOUTH

I dun' broke my chains and escaped to the North!

NARRATOR

He was gonna meet his destiny before he met his maker . . .

YOUTH

King James Baldwin! Queen Josephine Baker!

NARRATOR

They blazed his trail when they stepped outta line . . .

YOUTH

They owned Paris and Amsterdam's gonna be mine!

NARRATOR

He was born again. See, the real was at hand.

YOUTH

Oh, Hallelujah, I'm standin' on the Promised Land!

NARRATOR

*It was like they'd been expecting him,
Like they knew he was on the way,
Those casually enlightened regulars
Here at the Headquarters Café . . .*

43

CHRISTOPHE

So, do you play jazz?

JOOP

Do you play duh blues?

YOUTH

Do you live in a fucking windmill? Do you wear clog shoes?

CHRISTOPHE

You should play here at Headquarters.

JOOP

Is Titia still out of town?

MARIANNA

Where do you stay tonight?

NARRATOR

The wire got connected . . .

YOUTH

I guess I'll find a hotel . . .

NARRATOR

The mistake got corrected . . .

MARIANNA

A hotel? Pfff, don't you know where you are?

NARRATOR

Then she made him understand.

MARIANNA

We're your new family, man!

SONG: "KEYS"

Hey, Mr. L.A., I know a place that you can stay.
Right next door to here is a nice flat, yeah, it's OK.
The roommate's gone to Spain.
The place is sloppy, it's insane.

But the sun shines through big windows,
Only Dracula would complain.

No one's ever there, you'll have your peace.
There's a view and a bottle of gin.
She's back in, oh, two or three weeks,
Her room would be all yours till then.

So here's the keys . . .

YOUTH

Oh, you mean . . . ?

MARIANNA

My keys.

YOUTH

Wow. I mean . . .

MARIANNA

Here is my address.
You see, it's really quite a mess.
But take them, please.
My keys.

I got an extra set back at the place,
So take mine now, that's just in case you'll need
My keys,
My keys . . .

NARRATOR

She had a crazy mixed-up flat,
He wasn't thinking about that.
You know the bed was kinda hard,
A prison cot cum yoga mat.

Ten thousand paintings everywhere,
She was kind of an acrobat.
Oh, you were lucky to find a chair,
The sweetest dump in which he'd sat!

She had nude photos everywhere,
From freaky deeky to plain arty.

Some of her girlfriends showered there,
As you can see, Amsterdam's a party!

YOUTH

I appreciate this more than you could ever know. I promise I won't break a thing.

MARIANNA

Don't promise—you never know!
My place ain't all that wonderful,
But I hope you find it comfortable,
So please, take my keys.

The faucets leak, the cupboard's bare,
My underwear are everywhere,
But please, take my keys,
Take my keys.

YOUTH

And after so long feelin' so alone,
I feel like picking up the phone
And calling up that place called home,
To say I found a brand new family,
Where I can be that thing called "me."

No more saying "uncle" to Uncle Sam.
I'm telling L.A. just where I am.
Color me Amsterdam,
Amsterdam . . .

NARRATOR

So after a little conversation,
He's got keys to her flat.
After a little conversation,
He just walks across her welcome mat.

Now who woulda thought trust could be bought
For a song and a little chat?
See, he had friends and family
Nowhere near as cool as that.
She gave him these . . .
Her keys . . .

Now in Beverly Hills, they gave him chills.
And South Central put his soul in the deep freeze.
But she gave him her keys.

You know those L.A. ladies in their Mercedes,
They locked their doors if he'd just sneeze.
Now he's like, "Bitch, please . . .
She gave me her keys!"

He said, "The kinda place I wanna be
Is where no one's cold or scared of me."
And then she handed him these,
Her keys.

Yeah, I guess no one ever made him feel as real
As when she mended him,
By lending him her keys.

And said:
Welcome to Amsterdam,
Welcome to Amsterdam,
Welcome to Amsterdam.

She said: "Hey, it might look like Sodom
From top to bottom,
A shopping mall of vice,"
But it was all right with me now.

BAND

Yeah, it's alright.

NARRATOR

Cuz she said it's alright.

BAND / ALL

Yeah, it's alright.

NARRATOR

She said, "Yeah, it might look like Sodom
From top to bottom,
A shopping mall of vice . . ."
But it was all right with me now.

BAND / ALL

Yeah, it's alright.

NARRATOR

Cuz she said it's alright.

BAND / ALL

Yeah, it's alright.

(NARRATOR *does that crazy ad-lib thing, which goes on for awhile.*)

NARRATOR

Welcome to Amsterdam!

YOUTH

It's alright with me, yeah . . .
"It may look like Sodom and Gomorrah . . .
But who could ask for . . . more-a."
Shit!

MARIANNA

Are we disturbing the moment of creation?

RENATA

"The Moment of Creation." My God, Marianna, songwriting is a job like any other!

MARIANNA

It's a sacred calling!

RENATA

It doesn't make you special.

MARIANNA

I ask you: who can fathom the mysteries of music?

YOUTH

(*Really going with it.*)

It's a fathomless mystery, yeah! Often I feel as if it's the song that's writing me!

(RENATA *laughs.*)

MARIANNA

Hey—tell me your secret. Where, I ask you, where do songs come from?

SONG: "WE JUST HAD SEX"

NARRATOR

Open up the flood gates,
Knock down all your fences,
The real is just around the corner,
Test drive your new senses.

Unfetter, un-sweater, it's wetter,
And it just keeps getting
Better and better and better and better . . .

MARIANNA

We just had sex.
There's nothing sleazy 'bout
A natural reflex.
It's nice and easy.
No need to crane your necks.
It's all cool breezy, baby.
What's a little bedroom traffic?
Evening News is pornographic!

RENATA

We just had sex.

YOUTH / MARIANNA / RENATA

That's right: all three of us.

RENATA

It's not complex.

YOUTH / MARIANNA / RENATA

It's no big deal at all.

RENATA

We'll smoke cigarettes
And probably talk about:

MARIANNA

Ten or fifteen things,

RENATA

Before anyone brings up the fact that:

MARIANNA / RENATA

We just had sex.
To keep it fresh sometimes
We shuffle the decks.
We realize that this might
Fog up your specs,
But that's just how it goes.

RENATA (*Cont'd.*)

You might find it quite risqué,

MARIANNA

But it's the European way!

YOUTH / MARIANNA / RENATA / JOOP / CHRISTOPHE

Don't get too vexed,
It's really no big deal
That we just had sex.
And now we're gonna roll five big cigarettes,

MARIANNA / RENATA / JOOP / CHRISTOPHE (*Cont'd.*)

And have a cup of coffee.

YOUTH

I LOVE how they're so nonchalant about the only thing I want!

NARRATOR

The pilgrim crossed both land and sea to find a cathedral home,
Then two girl Jesuses colored him Lazarus and rolled away the
stone.

YOUTH

Dear Mr. Franklin: Today I don't feel as ugly as I did yesterday.
In high school gym showers I crouched in shame like Adam in
the garden, but this morning in Amsterdam I was ten foot tall on
a movie screen staring down at myself in the back row. Today
in Amsterdam I sat before her as she explained the history of

Dutch colonialism without her shirt on. Today in Amsterdam their tobacco mouths tasted like sweet blood oranges. Today in Amsterdam I learned how to pronounce their last names, lost track of how many times I came and stared out of windows and nothing was the same. Today in Amsterdam the unspeakable beauty of overflowing ashtrays, espresso gone cold and a half-smoked joint on the table awed me. Today in Amsterdam the charcoal drawing she made of me naked doesn't look as ugly as I felt yesterday. This is the real city of angels. They remade me in their image . . . Did I say already, Mr. Franklin, that today in Amsterdam they taught me how to wear my body? Today I learned that even if it's ugly, man, you gotta wear it like a gown.

    (Beat.)

Now I can write some real songs . . .

MOTHER
He writes his own songs, you know.

SONG: "STONED"

NARRATOR
He measured time passing in hits from the bong,
All day café hangs, and unfinished songs.
Then her keys weighed more than the axe in his hand,
When he tried to write a song,
He knew she wouldn't understand.

MOTHER
It's such a beautiful Sunday morning!

YOUTH
She's living in a phony paradise . . .
No, wait . . .
So many things she doesn't realize . . .
She's . . . basking in hell's . . . sunshine . . .
How does this song go?

MOTHER
He's just going through a phase. Even "artists" have to grow up!

NARRATOR

He's trying to write a song,
But the song is writing him,
It's a song about paradise
Wearing thin.

MOTHER

After all, a real man doesn't ignore his loved ones, no sir.

YOUTH

Today paradise was the enemy,
Today the real became routine,
Today my edges dulled together.
Yeah, that's it!
And there's no point left to dream
I wanna SCREAM . . .

Mamaaaaaaa, Marianna and Moroccan hash have got me stoned,
And I can't find my way home.
Mamaaaaaaa, she's serving ev'ry one of my desires
On a platter,
But it doesn't even matter anymore.
Oh-oh, paradise is a bore,
It doesn't even matter anymore.

Oh-oh, paradise is a bore . . .

YOUTH (*Cont'd.*) **/ NARRATOR**

It doesn't even matter anymore . . .

NARRATOR (*Cont'd.*)

Ah, paradise is a bore . . .
You get it?

YOUTH

Yeah, I got it.

MARIANNA

I thought everything was alright . . .

YOUTH

It's hard to write songs when you're already in paradise.

MARIANNA

Ah, so I see the problem.

YOUTH

It's like I can't get too comfortable. Otherwise I'll forget all the shit there is to complain about.

(HE *is dead serious.* SHE *thinks it's a hoot.*)

MARIANNA

How wonderfully neurotic! It's good yer going to Berlin—you'll fit right in!

YOUTH

You're making this so easy for me.

MARIANNA

Why make things hard?

YOUTH

Well, *here's your keys . . .*

NARRATOR

Keys to her city opened his floodgates, he followed her river's weave . . . the same keys that gave him the power to stay . . . now gave him the courage to leave . . . she gave him these . . .

MARIANNA

You know, there's so much more to Amsterdam than hash bars and squatted houses. One day maybe you'll know the real city.

YOUTH

So if Berlin sucks, I can come back to you.

MARIANNA

No.

NARRATOR

No one ever made him feel as real
As when she mended him by lending him . . .

YOUTH

Hey, I gotta leave.

NARRATOR

Her keys . . .

MARIANNA

Right when it was starting to feel real.

CHORUS

Why you wanna leave right when it was starting to feel real?
Why you wanna leave right when it was starting to feel real?

YOUTH

It doesn't even matter anymore . . .

CHORUS

Why you wanna leave right when it was starting to feel real?

YOUTH

Paradise is a bore,
It doesn't even matter anymore . . .

CHORUS / BAND

Why you wanna leave right when it was starting to feel real?

YOUTH

Paradise is a bore . . .

CHORUS / BAND

Why you wanna leave right when it was starting to feel real?
Why you wanna leave right when it was starting to feel real?
Why you wanna leave . . .

NARRATOR

(*Speaking over* CHORUS.)

O daisy chain of soulful days,
Goodbye, city of Amsterdam.
Sometimes the melody's goin' one way,
But then the song has other plans.

We're gonna take a little break right now, then come back with
all to reveal . . .

CHORUS
Right when it was starting to feel real?

(Blackout.)

End of Act One

Act Two

Berlin:
A Black Hole with Taxis

NARRATOR

Berlin: A black hole with taxis.
Berlin: A forest of sharp corners.
Berlin: Swallowed if harmful . . .
It was two miles from right,
It was always all night.
A concrete pool that kept diving into you blind.
Berlin was always creeping up from behind.

(YOUTH *is startled by East German* BORDER GUARD.)

BORDER GUARD

Ausweiss!!!

YOUTH

Huh?

BORDER GUARD

Identity! Your identity!!!

YOUTH

My identity?

BORDER GUARD

Pass!

(YOUTH *attempts to pass him.* BORDER GUARD *grabs him,
really pissed.)*

PASS!!!

YOUTH

I don't understand—

BORDER GUARD

Give-Me-Your-PASS-PORT!

(Riot erupts. The NOWHAUS COLLECTIVE *storms the stage, screaming, yelling, throwing rocks at cops, i.e., audience.)*

SONG: "MAY DAY"

NARRATOR

May Day,
May Day, there's a riot going down,
In a deep, dark corner of West Berlin town.
May Day,
May Day, there's a riot going down,
In a deep, dark corner of West Berlin town.

NARRATOR / BAND

May Day,
May Day, there's a riot going down,
In a deep, dark corner of West Berlin town!
MAY DAY, MAY DAY, THERE'S A RIOT GOING DOWN!!!
IN A DEEP, DARK CORNER OF WEST BERLIN TOWN!!!

Meet Nowhaus

HUGO

Narrative is a capitalist plot!

NARRATOR

Meet Hugo, bitter music critic and part-time bartender. He poured a mean Molotov cocktail . . .

HUGO

Pop music is the religion of the opiated! And zat means you, fascist piggies!!!

SUDABEY

Make movies, not love!!!

NARRATOR

And here's Sudabey, post-modern pornographer and social critic.

SUDABEY

(To YOUTH.*)*

I greet you. My porno films feature fully clothed men making business deals.

YOUTH

Yeah, that sounds hot.

NARRATOR / BAND

Molotov cocktails are turning up the heat,
And the overturned cars are burning in the street,
And the people keep on screaming,
And the billy clubs are swinging,
And the people keep on screaming,
And the billy clubs are swinging.

YOUTH

What the fuck is going on?
What the fuck is going wrong?
Can I get a straight answer . . . ???

NARRATOR

Check the chorus of this song:

NARRATOR / BAND / NOWHAUSERS

May Day, May Day, there's a riot going down!
May Day, May Day, there's a riot going down!
May Day, May Day, there's a riot going down!
May Day, May Day, there's a riot going down!

NARRATOR

And then she came . . . to the rescue. . .

*(*DESI *emerges phoenix-like from the ashes of the melee.)*

Ooooo-weee, Ms. Desi, that is. Desi Desi, that is. She was a left-wing love machine. Can you dig it? She was uptight, outta sight. "Workers of the world unite!!!"

BAND / NOWHAUSERS

"Workers of the world unite."

NARRATOR / BAND

All night.

NARRATOR

Until you get it right—

DESI

(Interrupts NARRATOR.)

Have a discussion with ze hand! A woman can speak for herself.

HEIDI

Yeah. That's right.

DESI

Ich bin Desi. Welcome to our riot.

NARRATOR

And when Desi started talkin', everybody got quiet . . .

DESI

I am the founder of Nowhaus,
The home where Life becomes Art.
It's a halfway house, I guess you could say,
For those who have to live life more than halfway.

I don't write or paint or sculpt, you see,
My masterpiece is this family.
I've built this radical sanctuary,
Where only love is revolutionary.

YOUTH

Hey, whatta you say after this riot we grab ourselves a little drink and—

NARRATOR

Hey man!
Nowhaus was not looking for your Real.

BAND

Nowhaus was not looking for the Real.

NARRATOR

Nowhaus built the real with their ideals.

BAND

Nowhaus built the real with their ideals.

NARRATOR

Nowhaus was not looking for your real.

BAND

Nowhaus was not looking for the real.

NARRATOR

Nowhaus built the real with their ideals.

BAND

Nowhaus built the real with their ideals.

NARRATOR

And then the sirens sang a hymn to him
To frame this episode
They sang: "Are you ready?"

BAND / NOWHAUSERS

Yeah!

NARRATOR

"Are you ready?"

BAND / NOWHAUSERS

Yeah!

NARRATOR

"Are you readyyyy?"

BAND / NOWHAUSERS

Yeah!

BAND / NOWHAUSERS / NARRATOR

To explooooode!!!!!!!!!!!!!!!!!

(We hear a low discordant menacing drone, bordering on the
genuinely annoying.)

SONG: "SURFACE"

NARRATOR

And then the billy clubs stopped swinging,
And the police held their breath . . .

MR. VENUS

What's inside is just a lie.

NARRATOR

Molotov cocktails cops could handle,
But performance art scared them to death.

MR. VENUS

What's inside is just a lie.

NARRATOR

And then the frontline of the uprising became a gilded stage.

MR. VENUS

What's inside is just a lie.
There's only surface.

NARRATOR

Welcome to Mr. Venus' Riot Cabaret!

MR. VENUS

What's inside is just a lie.
What's inside is just a lie.
What's inside is just a lie.
What's inside is just a lie . . .

Ideas are dependable, there's a new one every week.
Emotions are expendable because they aren't unique.

Ideas are dependable, there's a new one every week.
Emotions are expendable because they aren't unique.

Culture is cosmetic!!!
Culture is cosmetic!!!
Culture is cosmetic!!!
Culture is cosmetic!!!

What's Inside Is Just a Lie.
What's Inside Is Just a Lie.
What's Inside Is Just a Lie.
WHAT'S INSIDE IS JUST A LIE!!!

NARRATOR

Now, say your songs sounded like this:

YOUTH

Don't try to hide . . .
The truth is inside . . .

NARRATOR

And then you heard this . . .

MR. VENUS

WHAT'S INSIDE IS JUST A LIE!!!

NARRATOR

It would have to make some kinda impression on you, now
wouldn't it?
Or in other words . . .
His song was ugly, cold and cracked,
But Venus had something our hero lacked:

YOUTH

Courage to bleed . . .

NARRATOR

Venus gave him . . .

(MR. VENUS *and* YOUTH *snort speed in unison.*)

SPEED!!!

OK, and I know this is gonna sound a little bit crazy, but
according to the Nowhaus manifesto and I quote: "What's
inside of each and every one of us here in this room, what we
mistakenly call *our* thoughts, *our* feelings and *our* dreams, have
actually been put there by a system, therefore . . ."

MR. VENUS

What's inside is just a lie . . .

NARRATOR

Our minds have been invaded, conquered and occupied. Hence:

MR. VENUS

What's inside is just a lie.

NARRATOR

And like a catchy refrain that gets trapped in your head . . .

MR. VENUS

What's inside is just a lie.

NARRATOR

Like a catchy refrain that gets trapped in your head . . .

MR. VENUS

What's inside is just a lie.

NARRATOR

Somebody else's desires get lodged in your brain . . .

MR. VENUS

What's inside is just a lie.

NARRATOR

And so the only way to become your true self . . .

MR. VENUS

What's inside?

YOUTH

I'm starting to feel real . . .

NARRATOR

You gotta create your true self.

MR. VENUS

What's inside?

YOUTH

I'm starting to feel real . . .

MR. VENUS

What's inside?

NOWHAUSERS

(Chant.)

We wish to create an anti-bourgeois living community
That stands in opposition to capitalist society.

NARRATOR

You turn your life into a work of art.
You turn your life into a work of art.
You turn your life into a work of art.
You turn your life into a work of art!

MR. VENUS

What's inside?

YOUTH

I'm starting to feel real. I'm starting to feel real. I'm starting to
feel real. I'm starting to feel real. I'm starting to feel real. I'm
starting to feel real. I'm starting to feel real.

MR. VENUS

What's inside is just a lie!!!!

(All of the above statements repeat in chants. MUSIC builds
into mass swirl of voices . . . YOUTH, in a fit of riot-fueled
adrenalin and testosterone, kisses DESI, not romantic but
impulsive.)

YOUTH

So the Real that I've been searching for . . .
Is in the beauty of these burning streets.
It's the song I couldn't write yesterday.

MR. VENUS

What's inside is just a lie!!!!

YOUTH

Till May Day gave me the courage to bleed . . .

DESI
Only love is real, yeah . . .

YOUTH
I'll write a song called revolution.

MR. VENUS
What's inside is just a lie!!! . . .

YOUTH
Cuz May Day gave me the courage to bleed.

DESI
Only love is real, yeah . . .

YOUTH
And now I'm ready,

BAND / ALL
YEAH!

YOUTH
And now I'm ready,

BAND / ALL
YEAH!

YOUTH
And now I'm ready,

BAND / ALL
YEAH!

BAND / ALL / YOUTH
To explode!

YOUTH
And now I'm ready,

BAND / ALL
YEAH!

YOUTH

And now I'm ready,

BAND / ALL

YEAH!

YOUTH

And now I'm ready,

BAND / ALL

YEAH!

YOUTH

To

BAND / ALL / YOUTH

Explode!

YOUTH

And now I'm ready,

BAND / ALL

YEAH!

YOUTH

And now I'm ready,

BAND / ALL

YEAH!

YOUTH

And now I'm ready,

BAND / ALL

YEAH!

YOUTH

To

BAND / ALL / YOUTH

Explode!

NARRATOR

Then they all walked back to Nowhaus,
Where the two sat down to tea.
Did I mention Desi and Hugo
Just broke up recently?

Well, anyway, life was revolutionary
And love was almost free.
And the riot, comrade, was you and . . .

YOUTH

. . . that riot was me. So this is where me and the real shall
meet. Not in some stupid little song . . . but in the middle of the
"Burning street where she lives . . ."

(DESI *and* YOUTH *at table.* NOWHAUSERS *perform various
activities in background that reflect their interests.)*

NARRATOR

When they weren't taking long afternoon walks by the Berlin
Wall, mornings and evenings found Desi and the new guest
taking tea in the Nowhaus rec room, where she would open up
the world and invite him inside . . .

DESI

The system wants us sick and unsatisfied so we'll mindlessly
consume their products and call that living. We're all damaged.
But here at Nowhaus we feel that healing and the smashing of
capitalism go hand in hand . . .

(SHE *holds his hand "platonically."*)

YOUTH

Healing?

DESI

. . . Art heals, man! When we are in the presence of Art . . .

(Brief pause.)

. . . we are taking the cure. And that's revolutionary. I don't know
how we'd manage without it.

SONG: "DAMAGE"

NARRATOR

She had an everyday solution
For the emptiness you'd feel.
She called it revolution.
She told him:

NARRATOR / DESI

. . . Only love is real.

NARRATOR (*Cont'd.*)

And days would pass and he would never know where Desi ended and Berlin began. He just knew that she was a new kind of music . . . the music of May Day, man.

DESI

You didn't know that 80% of the farming in Africa is done by women?

YOUTH

Uh . . . I don't even know who does 80% of the farming in America.

NARRATOR

In L.A., OK, the sun shines
Every single day of the year
But if you loved paradise's confines,
You wouldn't be sitting here . . .

And like the bank and the burned-down supermarket still smoldering in the distance, his American soul had been razed to the ground by Desi's irresistible mind. But out of the ashes of him arose a new soul, the soul of a young lion.

YOUTH

You cannot accuse third world men of being sexist when sexism itself is a Western concept!

DESI

Listen to you now!

YOUTH

We can't force our values on them! You can't ignore the cultural specifics.

DESI

Nazism was culturally specific to Germany. Should we have ignored it?

YOUTH

I walked right into that one, didn't I?

DESI

Yes, you did . . .

YOUTH

I started off pretty strong, though . . .

DESI

Yeahhhh . . . not really.

(BOTH *laugh*.)

NARRATOR

She was a riotous proposal,
She was an overthrow, a coup.
She said the day's at your disposal,
We can seize it, me and you.

. . . and he would steal her sweet blessings and bathe all night in her fire . . . But he never said thank you for quenching my desire . . . thank you for leading me through the flames, through the noise, through the chaos, through the dark night of your mind and your small hand guiding me through the teargas cloud, he never said . . . thank you for all the love she allowed . . . but he was thankful in his way: thankful for the music of May Day. And when the house grew quiet and the cigarette smoke curled between them in the lamplight, he'd find her more than beautiful, staring out the window, onto the street, almost whispering . . .

DESI

The system does all kinds of damage . . .

YOUTH

Ich Lieder dich . . .

DESI

Du liedst mich? Ha-ha . . . Baby, we need to work on your German!

YOUTH

What'd I say?

DESI

(Mocking, teasing, flirting.)

"What'd I say?"

NARRATOR

Only love is real, yeah . . .

DESI

(Laughing.)

Ich Lieder dich!

YOUTH

It means "I love you," right?

DESI

Lie-*ber* is love. "Lie-*der*" means song. You said, "I song you."

(THEY both laugh . . .)

NARRATOR

He depended on the music of May Day to heal.
Depended on Desi to touch, see and feel.
But we'll never know exactly just what was the deal,
Whether he heard her or not when she said . . .

DESI

Only love is real . . .

NARRATOR

Did you hear her when she said . . .

DESI

Only love is real . . .

Only love is real . . .
Only love is real . . .
Only love is real . . .
Only love is real . . .

YOUTH

. . . it's about commitment to your *own* vision! And having the courage to bleed for it! One uncompromising vision! The orchestra conductor! The puppet master!

(Becoming increasingly hysterical.)

The super-revolutionary-artist must be prepared to trample all in his path to reach the final aesthetic conquest!

(Now totally over the top.)

The whole fucking world as my own multi-media spectacle! Mere mortals mate! But only gods like us create!!!

(MUSIC out.)

HUGO

You need to create a place to stay tomorrow. Your guest period is now over. *Auf wiedersehen.*

YOUTH

What do you mean? I'm an artist too! I belong here!

HUGO

Nowhaus is a family of art revolutionaries. And you really don't seem like a team player.

MR. VENUS

Look, Mr. American Pop Song Maker: if your songs do not critique the hegemony of populist consumption . . .

SUDABEY

Or if they mimic the phallocentric narrative of verse chorus verse chorus climax fade out smoke a cigarette turn over snore all night and never call me again . . .

HUGO

Then they are nothing more than tools of the oppressor . . .

YOUTH

Wait a minute!!! Rock and roll: a tool of the oppressor? What about the Clash?

SPURNEY

Yeah, man!
The Clash! Sandinista . . .

HUGO

Punk rock was a marketing strategy.

SUDABEY

And what about zat Dutch girl singing about her fucking keys . . .

HUGO

Good for her, she has a nice flat . . .

MR. VENUS

Heterosexual love lacks drama!

HEIDI

That's bullshit.

(*Swirling debate ensues . . .* BAND *and* NOWHAUSERS *pair up into discussion teams. Dialogue overlaps.*)

NARRATOR

(*Over the noise.*)

Welcome to an average day among the Nowhaus tribe. This little discussion lasted for two whole weeks until finally—

HUGO

Look, let's cut to ze chase scene, ja? Please give us one reason why we should allow you to stay.

YOUTH

Um . . . because I'm black?

ALL
What's that?

YOUTH
(*To* HUGO.)

Yeah, Mr. May 68: do you know what it's like to be the object of oppression living under police occupation in the ghetto?

NARRATOR
He did not. His police-occupied ghetto looked more like . . .

(MOTHER *enters.*)

MOTHER
Your friend Terry stopped by again in that *brand-new* Datsun 240Z. He's making good money. And he's not even in a gang!

YOUTH
(*Emboldened, to* HUGO.)

Well, let me ask you this, Mr. Know-It-All: do you know what it's like to hustle for dimes on the mean streets of South Central?

NARRATOR
Nobody in this play knows what it's like to hustle for dimes on the mean streets of South Central. His mean streets looked more like . . .

MOTHER
I ran into Sherry at the arts and crafts fair. Boy, has she turned into a beautiful young lady. And as you know, she is NOT a crack ho.

YOUTH
(YOUTH *cues the funky "black"* MUSIC.)

Ever hear of the Projects?

MOTHER
This *palatial two-story house* feels empty without you!

YOUTH

They call it the Projects cuz we all workin' on a project called
"Just trying to live . . . to see tomorrow!"

MOTHER

And I'm working on a project called *"furniture re-upholstering*
for this wonderfully spacious, almost paid-for house . . ."

YOUTH

NOBODY knows the trouble I've seen! NOBODY! I come from
hell on earth: Illiteracy—guns—drugs—insanity—decay—

MOTHER

I wish you'd call me sometime.

YOUTH

And death.

(MOTHER *exits.*)

And I am no mere *popsongmaker.* I am an artist. My work is
about re-invention. My work is about . . . transcendence. My
work is about . . . the limits of blackness.

(YOUTH *does James Brown spin, capping it with a . . . HEY!!!*
EVERYONE *except* DESI *flinches . . .)*

HUGO

(Accepting defeat.)

Welcome to Nowhaus, comrade.

DESI

So blackness is the main subject of your work?

YOUTH

(Caught off-guard.)

Uhhh . . . Yes and no.

(Finds his footing.)

In other words . . . "yo."

75

NARRATOR

Cast your eyes to the center ring
Of a chilly arts space in the Nowhaus scene!
Only the transgressors can take this chance,
Only the guest listed can enter this trance.
In a metal skirt of bananas,
He gon' do his song and dance!

Strip your mind naked, pilgrim.
It's an opening, so take it, pilgrim.
Like Josephine Baker, don't fake it, pilgrim!

DESI

Knock 'em dead, my ghetto warrior!

NARRATOR

Just dance! Dance! Dance!

MR. VENUS

Meine Damen und "Herrings," in the most anticipated Berlin debut in recent memory, I force on you—Mr. Middle Passage!

SONG: "IDENTITY"

YOUTH

I am bleeding sunshine.
I am emptying my veins.
And when I'm done bleeding sunshine,
This song will break my chains.

Your gaze completes my being,
But I'll make you gaze in vain.
I illuminate with fiction,
The darkness truth cannot explain.

America is flowing,
Slowly exiting my veins.
I am giddy, cold and glowing,
And this song will break my chains.

The chains of I-i-i-i-i-i-i-dentity.
The chains of I-i-i-i-i-i-i-dentity.
The chains of I-i-i-i-i-i-i-dentity.

MOTHER

Why don't you want to be around your own people?

YOUTH

The key to the real is finally in my hand!
And now your expectations are exiting my veins!
The key to the real is finally in my hand!
And all your expectations are flowing out my veins!

Hit the wall, free at last!
Hit the wall, free at last!

I am the twentieth century incarnate!
Hit the wall, free at last!
The twentieth century coming home covered in mud,
And missing a shoe!

Child, what's become of you, haven't you got any sense?
Child, what's become of you, haven't you got any sense?
Child, what's become of you, haven't you got any sense?

Nein, Mama. Nein, Mama. Nein, Mama. Nein, Mama. Nein, Mama,
Mama, Mama, Mama, Mama . . .

   (Pause.)

Mutti . . . Bist du da? Hal-lo . . .

   (Pause.)

Mutti, kannst du ein bisschen geld fur mich senden? Hal-lo!
Mutti! Wir haben ein bad connection . . . wir haben ein bad
connection . . . wir haben ein bad connection . . . wir haben ein
bad connection . . . connection . . . connection . . . connection . . .
connection . . .

MOTHER

Why don't you want to be around your own people?

YOUTH

My pain and my ego
Once stood at opposing ends,
But they met up in Berlin,

Now they're the best of friends!

And now I'm drained of your expectations!
I was instructed from the heart
To let my pain fuck my ego,
And I call the bastard "art!"

PAIN!! EGO!! ART!!
PAIN!! EGO!! ART!!

I let my . . .

NARRATOR / BAND

Pain!

YOUTH

Fuck my

NARRATOR / BAND

Ego!

YOUTH

And I

NARRATOR / BAND

Call the bastard . . .

YOUTH

Art. I let my . . .

NARRATOR / BAND

Pain!

YOUTH

Fuck my

NARRATOR / BAND

Ego!

YOUTH

And I

NARRATOR / BAND

Call the bastard . . .

YOUTH

Art. I let my . . .

NARRATOR / BAND

Pain

YOUTH

Fuck my

NARRATOR / BAND

Ego

YOUTH

And I

NARRATOR / BAND

Call the bastard . . .

(MUSIC*: Big blues ending.*)

MR. VENUS

Only the slums of America could produce such pain.

HUGO

His ghetto angst is far superior to ours.

SUDABEY

Exquisite *(Pause.)* like an orgasm in reverse.

MR. VENUS

We love you . . . like an anthropologist loves a tribe.

YOUTH

Tribes must love the attention. I bet it makes them feel like stars!

SONG: "THE BLACK ONE"

NARRATOR

Who lends the club that speakeasy air?

The black one, the black one!
Who dances like a god and has "wunderbar" hair?
Der Schwarze!

Now he's the life of every soiree!
He'll give the bum's rush to your ennui.
Turn up these lights cuz I barely can see
The black one.

Is he the post-modern lawn jockey sculpture?

DESI
(Cynical, disapproving.)

The black one . . .

NARRATOR
The black one!
Or just a soul on a roll exploding your culture?
That black one!

YOUTH
An artist creates surfaces.

NARRATOR
And then comes the fee.
He's doing the same thing.

YOUTH
Except I call the surface me.

DESI
He's dancing in a cage.

YOUTH
But I'm the one with the key.

NARRATOR
And he's the Black One!

NARRATOR
He's the real voice of America,
And Berlin listened closely.

Speaking as a Negro from there-ica.
He was automatically . . .

YOUTH	DESI
Am I real now?	*Is he real now?*

NARRATOR

An expert on its evils.

YOUTH	DESI
Can I feel now?	*Can he feel now?*

NARRATOR

An authority on its crimes.

YOUTH	DESI
Am I real now?	*Is he real now?*

NARRATOR

And he could wax lyrical,
His knowledge was almost empirical,
Of oppression from the present back to slavery times.

YOUTH

Hot-cha-cha-cha-cha-cha-cha-cha-cha-cha-cha . . .

NARRATOR / ALL BUT YOUTH

Who lets us know that we're in the right place?
The Black One, the Black One.

Who's got "good times" painted right on his face?
The Black One!

He's living truth cuz his life is a dare,

In L.A. he had two left feet,
Our Berlin Fred Astaire!

He's so down to earth
When he's moonwalking on air.

DESI

Just cuz he's the Black One.

YOUTH

I'm the ghetto warrior, yeah!!!

NARRATOR

Oh, the L.A.P.D. never thought he was that cute,
But now a squad of ice queens are in hot pursuit.

YOUTH

I'm Superfly in the buttermilk!

DESI

(Suspicious.)

And we find him sehr gut.

YOUTH

Cuz I'm the Black One.

SUDABEY

I envy you so much!!! I want to be re-incarcerated as a black man!!!

NARRATOR

Oh, yeah!

(MUSIC *stops.*)

DESI

Why do you lie about who you are?

YOUTH

What?

DESI

This ghetto warrior persona—it's not you.

YOUTH

Look, black people go through hell every fucking day in America.

DESI

I know that.

YOUTH

And you will never understand the hell I'm from!

DESI

But remember the story you told me about your grandma, the one who had to pass in order to get a job? Well, I think you are passing for ghetto.

SONG: "COME DOWN NOW"

HEIDI

Listening is waiting . . .

DESI

You came here to be real . . . but yer not.

HEIDI

Listening is waiting . . .

DESI

How can I love you if I don't even know you?

HEIDI

Now you are knee deep in your head's footnotes.

DESI

Let me see your pain.

HEIDI

I'll take your complex out of context . . .

DESI

Let me know the geography of your hell.

I've been listening to you talking in your sleep,
It's a strange poetry.
You're always running from something, it seems.

Let me chase away whatever's hurting you,
Just have to ask it of me,
My love is more real than all your dreams.

DESI (Cont'd.)	HEIDI
'Cause I been thinking	Thinking 'bout leaving.
about leaving	
My fingerprints on your being,	Thinking 'bout leaving.
I've been thinking about leaving	Thinking 'bout leaving.
My fingerprints on your being,	Thinking 'bout leaving.
I been thinking about leaving	Thinking 'bout leaving.
My fingerprints on your being.	Thinking 'bout leaving.
It's like church now.	Leaving . . .

So come down now, remove your mask,
See, all you gotta do is ask me.
I'll give you all the love life allows.

So come down now, remove your mask,
See, all you gotta do is ask me.
I'll give you all the love life allows.

DESI / HEIDI

All you gotta do is ask me,
All you gotta do is ask me,
All you gotta do is ask me,
All you gotta do is ask me,
All you gotta . . .

DESI / HEIDI	NARRATOR
Do is ask me . . .	What does this feeling mean to you?
	Both to be seen and to be seen through?
All you gotta do is ask me,	What does this feeling mean to you?
All you gotta	
Do is ask me . . .	What does this feeling mean to you?
	Both to be seen and to be seen through?
All you gotta do is ask me,	
All you gotta	

HEIDI	NARRATOR
Do is ask me . . .	Love raged like an ocean in a state of withdrawal,
	A fishbowl of emotion and the Berlin Wall.
All you gotta do is ask me,	
	Love raged like an ocean in a state of withdrawal.
All you gotta do is ask me.	

DESI

Right when it is starting to feel real!

(DESI, NARRATOR *and* CHORUS *swirl together.)*

CHORUS

How you gonna deal?
Right when it was starting to feel real?
How you gonna deal?

NARRATOR

It was starting to feel real . . .

CHORUS

Right when it was starting to feel real?

HEIDI

All you gotta do is ask me,
All you gotta do is ask me,

CHORUS

How you gonna deal?

NARRATOR

It was starting to feel real . . .
To feel real . . .
To feel real . . .

HEIDI

All you gotta do is ask me,
All you gotta do is ask me,

CHORUS

How you gonna deal?

(PHONE *rings, cutting off the* MUSIC.)

Mom Phone Call

MOTHER

Did that jacket I sent fit alright?

YOUTH

The jacket? Uhhh, oh yeah, the jacket, yeah. It's fine, Mom. It's great. Snazzy.

MOTHER

I know you're picky but shoot, when it's cold a coat's a coat.

YOUTH

That's right.

NARRATOR

Home.

MOTHER

Well, seeing as how you didn't make it out last year, I know yer not gonna let me down this Christmas.

YOUTH

Let you down?

MOTHER

It'd be nice having you around, son. To talk.

YOUTH

But we're talking now, Mom.

MOTHER

Don't you miss the sunshine?

YOUTH

Whatta you wanna talk about?

MOTHER

Oh, you know, lots of things . . .

YOUTH

Like . . .

MOTHER

Um, well, I mean, first of all, you've been on this trip of yours for so long and . . .

YOUTH

Trip . . . ?

MOTHER

. . . and you're so hard to reach—

YOUTH

Mom, this is not a trip—

MOTHER

. . . and there are so many things we have to talk about . . .

YOUTH

I live here now.

MOTHER

. . . important things . . .

> (Beat. SHE *sort of winces as the realization of his last sentence hits her, then she recovers.)*

We have important things to talk about.

> (Pause.)

YOUTH

Mom . . . I live here now.

> (Silence.)

Did you hear me?

MOTHER

> (Firm, desperate, SHE *adopts a hint of the authoritarian Negro dialect mask as in the play's first scene, but subtle, not comical.)*

Now one thang you need to realize right here and now, son, is that I am impor—I mean—*your family* is important! You can't just sit over there and act like I—*like we don't exist!* Family is not some . . . some service you can take advantage of for twenty years and then cancel when it's convenient for you! It don't work like that!

YOUTH

I couldn't come back even if I wanted to.

MOTHER

Why not?

YOUTH

Why leave a place where I can be myself to come back to a place where I can't?

MOTHER

Why do you need a particular place to be yourself? Can't you be yourself at home?

YOUTH

No! Mom, I'm already 22! Life's passing me by! Los Angeles is just death row with palm trees. I'm scared of waking up one day and being . . .

MOTHER

Me?

YOUTH

. . . and not having lived the life I wanted to live.

MOTHER

Your deep concern for yourself is very moving . . .
it's touching, really.

YOUTH

Mom, you need to start focusing on other things besides me . . .
like your own life.

MOTHER

We need to talk, son.

YOUTH

I mean if I could focus on my art like you focus on me, I'd be Picasso by now. Besides, what's waiting for me in L.A., Mom?

(Long silence . . .)

OK, Mom . . . look . . . there's this show in Kassel that I gotta do in like, I don't know, two months or so . . . and it's big, really big . . . and then maybe sometime after that I can start thinking about when I can visit. Is that ok? Is that alright?

(Long pause.)

MOTHER
I love you.

YOUTH
But is that alright?

(Silence.)

Mom, I said I'll try to visit you as soon as I can. Is that alright?

(Silence.)

NARRATOR
You see, brothers and sisters, our hero, the fiery pilgrim, never saw the point of love without understanding.

MOTHER
(To NARRATOR.*)*

How 'bout now?

Home for Christmas

NARRATOR
It's Christmas time in Old Berlin,
And the snow is all about.
What could this mean to the Nowhaus scene?
The hero's about to find out . . .

YOUTH
One last piece of house business: I'm pleased to announce that my seven-hour composition "shower.hum.song" is finished!

NOWHAUSERS
Bravo! . . . Let's give it a spin! Turn it up! . . .

YOUTH
Not so fast. I've decided to unveil it on Christmas Day!

MR. VENUS
Christmas Day?

SUDABEY
Are you completely crazy?

YOUTH
I know, how embarrassingly Judeo-Christian of me. But it's not about the stupid holiday. It's about how I feel. Just being here is like Christmas to me. The song is just something for us to listen to while we party.

SUDABEY
No one is here for Christmas.

HUGO
We all go home for ze holidays.

YOUTH
Home?

SUDABEY
To our families in their sleepy West German villages.

HUGO
I am missing my stupid old friends.

SUDABEY
I cannot wait to lay around with my teddy bears.

HUGO
I love the look on my father's face when he serves the blood sausages. He remembers how I loved them as a child. But forgets I'm vegetarian!!!

(Only HUGO *laughs*.)

SUDABEY

You know, absence really does make ze heart grow into a state of mind which somehow transforms what you once could not stand about your family into a somehow quaint, pleasure-giving construct.

HUGO

Ain't it ze truth.

YOUTH

(To DESI.)

So you're leaving me here all alone?

DESI

You said you'd never be caught dead in my backwards little village.

MR. VENUS

With her backwards little parents . . .

DESI

It would be a nightmare for you.

HUGO

It would be a nightmare for your parents.

YOUTH

Why isn't your backwards little village a nightmare for you?

DESI

Why do you think I left?

YOUTH

I know why you left. I'm trying to figure out why you're going back.

DESI

One week out of the year I see my family. I'm sorry. But I don't want to take you.

YOUTH

You think I give a fuck about your little redneck village? I just can't believe you'd choose it over spending Christmas with me.

DESI

Scheisse, man, it's my family. It's Christmas.

YOUTH

(To MR. VENUS.*)*

Well, I guess it's just you and me, homeskillet. We'll hold the fort down. I mean this is Berlin, Goddamnit! Somebody's keeping it real for Christmas, ain't they?

MR. VENUS

I'm going home. Come, Hugo, come view my new blue leather mini-skirt.

HUGO

Why should I want to see your stupid . . .

SUDABEY

(To HUGO.*)*

Come see the Goddamn mini-skirt!

HUGO

(To YOUTH.*)*

True love can only exist after the revolution.

*(*VENUS, SUDABEY *and* HUGO *exit.)*

YOUTH

So much for me understanding the "geography" of *your* hell.

(Pause.)

DESI

When I visit my parents, I barely speak. There's an ocean between us. They don't know who I am or what I am doing. And they will never . . . ever . . . understand me.

YOUTH

So why be with people that don't understand you?

DESI

Because they love me . . .

YOUTH

That seven-hour piece was written for you.

DESI

I don't want to be a song. I want to be loved. And you don't know the difference.

(Pause.)

If you'd like to learn the difference, I'll stay.

YOUTH

It's not love if somebody has to change.

(Long pause.)

DESI

OK.

(DESI exits.)

MOTHER

(To YOUTH.)

I don't want to be a song.

NARRATOR

As snow began to fall, all Christmas Eve long, he worked through the night on one of them "Why'd She Leave Me?" songs.

SONG: "YOUTH'S UNFINISHED SONG"

YOUTH

Why leave me alone?
Her eyes were red,

But her heart's stone cold,
Why'd she go from me?

NARRATOR

He was soothed by the hush of snow-caked streets at dawn. His voice echoed in the ghost house all Christmas morning long.

YOUTH

I couldn't be her dream,
She focused on things
That weren't there in me,
Then she split the scene.

NARRATOR

And for once he wanted to be taken from his singing by his mother's Merry Christmas telephone ringing. But her call never came—and his song never ended.

YOUTH

She wanted me to change
That's not love in my view.
Let's inspect the remains
As she's alone now, too.

What's the point of looking
For what's not there in you?
You lose track of . . .
You lose . . .

How does this song go?

Da da da da da da da da da da da da . . .

SONG: "WORK THE WOUND"

NARRATOR

Every day I build a mask
Up to the task,
Another song, you see.

I live behind the rhyme and verse,
I lift my voice till I lift the curse,

It's all rehearsed, you see.

This music always rescues me,
There's a melody for every malady,
Prescription: Song, you see.

And should the mask begin to fall,
My chorus goes up like a twelve-foot wall,
So you can't see me . . .

And I'm blessed to entertain,
The crowd laughs and swoons.
It's loud guitars and champagne,
And I sleep well past noon.

But I've got a lot to explain,
To myself, not to you.
Like who lost track of her pain,
While working their wound?

YOUTH
Da da da da da da da da da da da da . . .

NARRATOR
So I finally found a home,
Between the clicks of a metronome,
In a song, you see.

Then I went out on a limb,
But the tree disappeared and the sky grew dim,
Then the song changed key.

But then you told me my pain entertained.
I heard the applause, thanking God you're sane,
But what about me?

See I'm cursed to entertain,
The crowd laughs too soon.
And all I have is my pain,
Sharp and way outta tune.

But I feel a bit ashamed
Since I'm still here marooned,

And you lose track of her pain
When yer working your wound.

And you lose track of her pain when you're working your wound,
And you lose track of her pain when you're working your wound.

And you lose track of her love,
And you lose track of her pain,
I just hop back on that train . . .
And keep working,
I keep working,
I keep working . . .

And that's how the song goes,
Yeah, that's how the fucking song goes,
Hey baby, that's how the song goes,
Ah, but the problem is it never stops.

You know it's weird when you wake up that morning and realize that your entire adult life was based on a decision made by a teenager. A stoned teenager.

I know there must be some investment bankers out there that know the feeling. Some time ago we had a dress rehearsal . . . it was free. Sorry I forgot to tell you about it. Anyway, we invited this guy whose offices are down on Lafayette and Astor. He sells pretzels. *(Pointing to first row center.)* We sat him in your seat. Afterwards we went to a bar and . . . after about 5 or 16 beers . . . he looked at me . . . and he said, "The Real." And I said, "Yeah." And he said, "The real is not real, my friend. The real is a construct. The real is a creation. The real is artificial. The kid in your play is looking for something in *life* . . . that can only be found . . . in art."

    (Pause.)

And I was like, "Damn, pretzel man. *(Pause.)* Yer a heavy motherfucker." *(Pause.)* Some people feel like art is more real than life . . . And that really gives you something to think about . . . especially if you're at a funeral . . .

    (The funeral happens. YOUTH *is at podium. Alone.)*

YOUTH

It's so great to see so many friends and family gathered here to
see my mother home.

(Pause.)

In the plane from Berlin back to L.A., I prayed for her to wait.
Long enough for me to see her again. Long enough for me
to . . . hear her again. Long enough for me to tell her I'm sorry.
And mean it . . .

(Pause.)

Last night I woke up in darkness. And I didn't know where I was.

(Pause.)

So I just sat there . . . asking her questions . . . all night
long . . . like how can I go on . . . when the love that kept me
aloft is gone?

(Pause.)

Well, now she's free . . . she made it home, I know. But now that
she left me . . . where am I to go?

(The MUSIC answers . . . sounding like the sun coming
up . . .)

YOUTH

I gotta fill this void inside me . . .

(The MUSIC answers even more insistent now: bigger,
brighter . . .)

Where am I to go . . . ?

(MUSIC swells with intensity: mallets, organ, bass, etc.)

I gotta fill the void with music . . .
I'll fill the void with song . . .
Till my cup runneth over . . .
All night long . . .

SONG: "PASSING PHASE"

I'll live in vans crammed with guitars.
I'll sleep on floors and play in bars.
I'll dance to my own metronome,
Till chaos feels like home.

I'll grow colder,
I'll grow bolder,
I'll grow older,
And keep fillin' my cup.

I'll grow colder,
I'll grow bolder,
I'll grow older,
But I'll never grow up.

YOUTH (*Cont'd.*)	**BAND**
And this is not a passing phase.	
	It was just a passing phase . . .
No, this is not a passing phase.	
	It was just a passing phase . . .
You see, I'll stay young for	
so long,	
	It was just a passing phase . . .
Till chaos feels like home.	
	It was just a passing phase . . .

YOUTH

Up and down from town to town,
Tour van wheels go round and round.
Up and down from town to town,
Tour van wheels go round and round.

Every night play rock and roll,
Get fucked up after the show,
In the morning lock and load,
And then leave . . .

(MUSIC *stops cold as* NARRATOR *interrupts and confronts*
YOUTH, *grabbing microphone.*)

NARRATOR

Right when it was starting to feel real . . .

Wish we could talk about
How the means will not prepare you for the ends,
How your epiphanies will become fair-weather friends,
How death will make you lower your defenses,
The only truth of youth is the grown-up consequences.

Song is a balm,
But Song cannot heal,
You believed in it too long,
Now I need something more . . .
I need something more than real.

Someday the chords of age
Will drown out the life you've been dreaming of.
Then you'll be out on your ass and cursing, alas,
Cuz your song is just passing for love.
Like my song was just passing for love.

And you will never see her again.
And I will never see her again.
And we will never see her again.

YOUTH

Is that it?

    (Beat.)

That's it? You know, you're right: you cannot bring her back. But why lose faith in the only thing that can? I will see her again . . . Because life is a mistake . . . that only art can correct. I will see her again . . . Every night . . . Cue music . . . Lights up on Mother in an outrageous gown . . . showing everyone.

MOTHER

What do you want me to say?

YOUTH

Tell him it's alright.

NARRATOR

Is it alright?

MOTHER

Don't be sad about your chosen path,
And where it's taken you thus far.
Cuz this is what you did,
And that is who you are.
And it's alright.

NARRATOR

Is it alright?

MOTHER

Yes, it's alright . . .

NARRATOR

Is it alright . . . ?

MOTHER

Yes, it's alright . . .

NARRATOR

Is it alright?

(MOTHER *and* YOUTH *exit.*)

SONG: "LOVE LIKE THAT"

I remember when I owned everything,
The sun and the moon and the rain,
And my domain
Stretched and yawned along the astral plain.

The universe is a toy in the mind of a boy,
And life is a movie too, starring you.
Your whole family's the cast and crew,
That's a little secret between God and you.

But ain't it strange how it all makes perfect sense,
Once your life becomes evidence
Of the need to feel

Love is more than real.

Because your mother's love might seem insane,
That's cuz she really knows everything.
Too bad it takes so long to see what you've been missing.

HEIDI
Love like that can't be measured anyway.

NARRATOR
Too bad it takes so long to see what you've been missing.

HEIDI
Love like that can't be measured anyway.

NARRATOR
Too bad it takes so long to see what you've been missing.

HEIDI
Love like that can't be measured anyway.

NARRATOR
Too bad it takes so long to see what you've been missing.

HEIDI
Love like that can't be measured anyway.

NARRATOR
Too bad it takes so long . . .

Cuz the Real is a construct . . .
It's the raw nerve's private zone . . .
It's a personal sunset . . .
You drive off into alone.

End of Act Two

Biographies

STEW is the critically acclaimed singer, songwriter, founder, and leader of The Negro Problem, a pop-rock combo from Los Angeles whose recordings include *Post Minstrel Syndrome* (1997), *Joys and Concerns* (1999), and *Welcome Black* (2002). Along with Heidi Rodewald, he co-founded the Afro-Baroque cabaret ensemble known as Stew. Their works include *Guest Host* (2000), *The Naked Dutch Painter* (2002), and *Something Deeper Than These Changes* (2003). He was an artist-in-residence at the California Institute of the Arts (2004–2005), Sundance Theater Lab (2004–2005), Sundance Screenwriters Lab (2005), and Sundance Directors Lab (2005). Stew is also the composer of "Gary Come Home" for the *SpongeBob SquarePants* cartoon.

Passing Strange, which Stew starred in and co-wrote with Heidi Rodewald, premiered at Berkeley Rep and the Public Theater (2006–2007) before transferring to Broadway in 2008. The show has been honored with the Drama Critics' Circle Award for Best Musical, the 2008 Obie Award for Best New American Theater Piece, and a Tony Award for Best Book of a Musical. Stew also received Tony nominations for Best Performance by a Leading Actor in a Musical, Best Original Score, and Best Orchestrations.

HEIDI RODEWALD has spent over a decade as a performer, arranger, producer, and composer for both The Negro Problem and the multi-disciplinary ensemble known as Stew. She is co-writer, with Stew, of *Passing Strange*, which was nominated for seven Tony Awards and won the 2008 Obie Award for Best New American Theater Piece. She composed music for *Karen Kandel's Portraits: Night and Day* (2004) and co-wrote with Stew the screenplay *We Can See Today* for the Sundance Screenwriters Lab/Directors Lab (2005). She wrote for and performed with seminal female punk band Wednesday Week.

Called "one of the most influential figures in the New York live-music business" by the *New York Times*, **BILL BRAGIN** is director of public programming for Lincoln Center, where he produces the popular Midsummer Night Swing and Lincoln Center Out of Doors festivals. Previously, he spent six years as director of Joe's Pub at the Public Theater, where he initiated *Passing Strange* and co-founded the annual globalFEST world music festival. Bragin has been artistic director of Central Park SummerStage, music curator at Symphony Space, and general manager of NYNO Records. He is music consultant for the TED Conferences, and he DJs internationally as "Acidophilus" with the GlobeSonic Sound System.